W9-CIJ-726

To Know God Better

To Know God Better

Compiled by *Winfred Rhoades*

Harper & Brothers
Publishers New York

TO KNOW GOD BETTER

Certain meditations and prayers appearing in this book are from the following copyrighted sources (see also pp. 203-210):

Altar Stairs by Joseph Fort Newton, copyright 1928 by The Macmillan Company.

The Beloved Community by Zephine Humphrey, copyright 1930 by E. P. Dutton & Co., Inc.

Christ in the Silence by C. F. Andrews, copyright 1933 by C. F. Andrews. Published by Abingdon Press.

Jesus and the Gospel of Love by Charles E. Raven, copyright 1931 by Henry Holt & Co., Inc.

Leaves from a Secret Journal by Jane Steger, copyright 1926 by Little, Brown & Co.

Letters by a Modern Mystic by Frank C. Laubach, copyright 1955 by Frank C. Laubach.

The Letters of William James edited by Henry James, copyright 1920 by Henry James. Published by Little, Brown & Co. and Atlantic Monthly Press.

Man Is Not Alone by Abraham Joshua Heschel, copyright 1951 by Abraham Joshua Heschel. Published by The Jewish Publication Society of America.

Meister Eckhart translated by Raymond Bernard Blakney, copyright 1941 by Harper & Brothers.

Out of My Life and Thought by Albert Schweitzer, copyright 1933 by Henry Holt & Co., Inc.

The Psychic Treatment of Nervous Disorders by Paul Dubois, copyright 1905 by Funk & Wagnalls Company.

Library of Congress catalog card number: 57-9890

TO THE READER

To know God better—that is what every individual in the world needs more than anything else: to know God more intelligently, more as a great personal experience, more as an enlightener and guide and strengthener, more as the source of confidence in life and in its meaning, more as the Everlasting Father in whom we live and move and have our being and from whom we may draw at any time and all the time light and guidance and power for the living of life as it ought to be lived.

God is an eternal mystery. Yet His presence can be felt, and multitudes of people have felt it; His voice can be heard inwardly, and multitudes of people have heard it; His strength can be drawn on, and those who have done so have found in themselves an ability to go ahead, and to continue going ahead, under conditions that had previously seemed impossible. The peace of God that passeth all understanding can become an experience even when desperate problems are in hand, and when decisions must be made which involve painful changes in one's entire way of life.

To help hungry hearts and troubled souls to know God better is the purpose of this book. When we know how straitened hearts and souls down through the centuries have learned to know God better, and how needy spirits have learned continually to live in strengthening relations with God, we ourselves can learn to enter into relations with Him more direct, more vital, and more stable than we have ever had before. Thus from St. Augustine in the fifth century to writers still living the selections in this book have been made.

Here are readings and prayers for two hundred days as well as Bible verses and suggested Scripture readings bearing upon each theme. It is hoped that the sources given in the back of the book will direct many to extend their reading to a fuller use of these masterpieces of devotion.

W. R.

To Know God Better

HOLY! HOLY! HOLY!

In the beginning God.   GENESIS 1:1

Read GENESIS 1:1-5

Did ever any other book in the world's long history open with words so sublime? *In the beginning God:* God before all things, God the Creator of all things, God above all things, God beneath all things, God round about all things, God making Himself manifest through all things. God always. Always God. God everywhere. God the Alpha and the Omega, the First and the Last. God the Father of all, over all and through all and in all. God the Father of the Lord Jesus Christ. God the Savior and Redeemer. God "whose glory fills the heaven." God "whose robe is the light, His canopy space." God who is at the same time "the Great Companion." God of whom Jesus said that He "is a Spirit, and they who worship him must worship him in spirit and truth."

PRAYER: *O thou Infinite and Eternal, in awe and adoration I lift up to Thee my mind and heart and soul. Help me today, and every day, to live with Thee and for Thee, in awareness of Thee and communion with Thee. To Thee be glory forever. Amen.*

I SHALL BE RESTLESS UNTIL—

The Lord is my portion, saith my soul. LAMENTA-
TIONS 3:24

Read I CHRONICLES 29:9-20

Great art Thou, O Lord, and greatly to be praised.
Thou madest us for Thyself, and our heart is restless, until it rest in Thee. I will seek Thee, Lord, by
calling on Thee; and I will call on Thee, believing
in Thee. My faith, Lord, shall call on Thee, which
Thou hast given me, wherewith Thou hast inspired me. What art Thou then, my God? What,
but the Lord God? Most highest, most good, most
potent, most omnipotent; most merciful, yet most
just; most hidden, yet most present; most beautiful,
yet most strong; stable, yet incomprehensible; unchangeable, yet all-changing; never new, never old;
all-renewing; ever-working, ever at rest; still gather-
ing, yet nothing lacking; supporting, filling, and
ever-spreading; creating, nourishing, and maturing;
seeking, yet having all things. And what have I now
said, my God, my life, my holy Joy? Oh! that I
might repose in Thee! Behold, Lord, my heart is
before Thee; open Thou the ears thereof, and *say
unto my soul, I am thy salvation.*

*Prayer: Deep calleth unto deep, O Lord: the
deep of my need unto the deep of thy Love. Enlighten Thou my eyes and my understanding lest I
fail in the great task of living. Amen.*

GOD THE SOUL'S JOY

I am Alpha and Omega, the beginning and the end, the first and the last.   REVELATIONS 22:13

Read REVELATION 22:12-14

I saw God above all things, above all my agitations which were no more than a grain of dust, above this present life, above the worlds, above the choirs of angels and of the Elect; God at the summit of Heaven. My soul joyed in His life, in His Eternity, in His Immensity. I saw God in Himself, God One, God in His Three Adorable Persons, and this life was beauty, goodness, and magnificence.... And God awaits the soul! What love! And from the moment she turns toward Him she finds Him. One single instant suffices for this ineffable union, this transport of love; place, time, and the company in which we find ourselves, are immaterial. . . . In that union *God makes the soul partake of His own Self;* she is nourished by His Substance.

PRAYER: *O Thou who art above all the agitations of my heart and soul, help me to walk always in awareness of Thee, and in mystic communion with Thee, and in profound union with Thee, and in quick responsiveness to Thee. In the name of Jesus Christ. Amen.*

HONEST SEEKING LEADS TO FINDING

Ye shall seek me, and find me, when ye shall search for me with all your heart.   JEREMIAH 29:13

Read JEREMIAH 29:1-14

"Thou wouldst not seek Me hadst thou not already found Me." . . . This thought struck me like a flash of light. It was the solution of a problem that had long appeared to be insoluble. . . . Revelation therefore is not a communication once for all of immutable doctrines which only need to be held fast. The object of the revelation of God can only be God Himself, and if a definition must be given of it, it may be said to consist of the creation, the purification, and the progressive clearness of the consciousness of God in man—in the individual and in the race.

PRAYER: *Infinite Father, the blessing I ask is that Thou wilt make me aware, through sense and circumstance and history, that my soul can be in communion with thy soul. Accept my thanksgiving and my praise, that I may know Thee and love Thee and so live in thy love and compassion as to have perfect peace as to the meaning of my life and the destiny of the world. Let nothing come between me and Thee, O thou perfect Father and Lover of men, let nothing come between me and Thee. Amen.*

GOD IN HIS SOVEREIGN BEAUTY

Thus the heavens and the earth were finished, and all the host of them. And on the seventh day God ended his work which he had made; and he rested on the seventh day from all his work which he had made.   GENESIS 2:1, 2

Read PSALM 19:1-6

The Beloved unveiled to me his Sovereign Beauty, and my soul was lost entirely in the light of it. I saw in Him all created beauty. I saw intellectual beauty. I saw moral beauty. I saw the beauty of order, of proportion, of immensity; the beauty of harmony, the beauty of form, of colour. I saw all these things, not in themselves and as we generally see them; I saw them *in their principle* which is the Divine Beauty, and I saw that infinite Beauty *Itself,* independently of all the beauty It had created, but I cannot express what It is, because I saw It, adored It, without comprehending It. That infinite Beauty appears to the soul in the Divine Essence incomparably superior to created beauty and like a splendour which nothing can ever express.

PRAYER: *O Lord, my God, I praise Thee for the arching sky and the blessed winds, for the driving clouds and the constellations on high. I praise Thee for the salt sea and the running water, for the everlasting hills, for the trees, and for the grass under my feet. I thank Thee for a mind to think with, and a heart to love with, and strength to work with. To Thee be glory. Amen.*

WE NEED THE LIVING GOD

Oh that I knew where I might find him! that I might come even to his seat!   JOB 23:3

Read JOB 4:1-21; 16:1-5

All our sacred books are of the God who was, of the splendor that appeared to other souls, of the tender mercy that made other lives bearable and beautiful. They are precious, they cleanse and enlarge the eye of the spirit; they set our needs and our privileges in the atmosphere of the noblest humanity; but they are instrumental and not final, they are the telescope and not the star. We seek not the report of God in the speech of men, but God Himself, the living God. We must behold for ourselves the Eternal Wonder and live in the awe and hope of his discovered and glorious Presence.

PRAYER: *O Thou Infinite and Eternal, who hast surrounded me with the beauty of the outer world in which I live, help me day by day to find Thee more clearly in those wonders, and, more than all else, in the inner realm of mind and heart and spirit where I may have deep communion with Thee. In the name of Jesus Christ. Amen.*

THE GLORIOUS PRESENCE

And the Lord God formed man of the dust of the ground, and breathed into his nostrils the breath of life; and man became a living soul.   GENESIS 2:7

Read GENESIS 2:4-7

One day I saw a flower and began to think about its fragrance and its beauty. As I thought more deeply, I saw the Creator behind his creation, though hidden from my gaze. This filled me with joy. But my joy was greater still when I found Him working in my own soul. I was led to exclaim: "Oh! how wonderful Thou art! Separate from Thy creation and yet ever filling it with Thy glorious presence."

PRAYER: *The glorious majesty of the Lord my God be upon me; prosper Thou the work of my hands upon me; oh, prosper Thou my handy-work. Lord, be Thou within me to strengthen me; without me to keep me; above me to protect me; beneath me to uphold me; before me to direct me; behind me to keep me from straying; round about me to defend me. Blessed be Thou, O Lord, our Father, for ever and ever. Amen.*

MY GREATEST NEED

When thou saidst, Seek ye my face; my heart said
unto thee, thy face, Lord, will I seek.   PSALM 27:8

Read PSALM 27:1-8

Throughout his life he [Tennyson] had a constant feeling of a spiritual harmony existing between ourselves and the outward visible Universe,
and of the actual immanence of God in the in-
finitesimal atom as in the vastest system. "If God,"
he would say, "were to withdraw Himself for one
single instant from this Universe, everything would
vanish into nothingness." When speaking on that
subject he said to me: "My most passionate desire is
to have a clearer and fuller vision of God. The soul
seems to me one with God, how I cannot tell. I
can sympathize with God in my poor little way."

PRAYER: *O my God, I praise and bless and love
and thank Thee, I praise and bless and love and
worship Thee, I praise and bless and love and
glorify Thee. Amen.*

9TH DAY

CREATION AND GOD

Lift up your eyes on high, and behold who hath
created these.   ISAIAH 40:26

Read JOB 38:1-12

I asked the earth, and it answered me, "I am not He"; and whatsoever are in it, confessed the same. I asked the sea and the deeps, and the living creeping things, and they answered, "We are not thy God, seek above us." I asked the air; and the whole air with his inhabitants answered, "Anaximenes was deceived, I am not God." I asked the heavens, sun, moon, stars, "nor (say they) are we the God whom thou seekest." And I replied unto all the things which encompass the door of my flesh: "Ye have told me of my God, that ye are not He; tell me something of Him." And they cried out with a loud voice, "He made us."

PRAYER: *Great and marvellous are thy works, Lord God Almighty; just and true are thy ways, Thou King of saints. Who shall not fear Thee, O Lord, and glorify thy name? for Thou only art holy: for all nations shall come and worship before Thee; for thy judgments are made manifest. Alleluia: for the Lord God omnipotent reigneth; let me be glad and rejoice, and give honour to Him. Amen.*

IOTH DAY

GOD KNOWN IN NEGATIVES

Is there a God beside me? yea, there is no God.
ISAIAH 44:8

Read ISAIAH 44:6-8

We know God more perfectly (says St. Diony-

9

sius) by Negatives, than by Affirmatives. We think more loftily of God, by knowing that He is incomprehensible, and above our understanding, than by conceiving Him under any image, and created beauty, according to our rude understanding. A greater esteem and love, then, will flow from this confused, obscure, and negative method than from any other which is sensible and distinct; because the former is more fitting to God and abstracted from Creatures; and the latter, on the contrary, the more it depends on Creatures, the less it hath of God.

PRAYER: *Holy and Infinite! Viewless! Eternal! Veiled in the glory that none can sustain, None comprehendeth thy Being supernal, Nor can the heaven of heavens contain. Glorious in holiness, fearful in praises, Who shall not fear Thee, and who shall not laud? Anthems of glory thy universe raises, Holy and Infinite! Father and God! Amen.*

11TH DAY

GOD IS EVERYWHERE

Thou, even thou, art Lord alone.   NEHEMIAH 9:6

Read NEHEMIAH 9:1-6

What is sometimes here and sometimes there is not everywhere, and above all things and places; so also, what is to-day, or to-morrow, is not always, at all times, and above all time; and what is some thing, this or that, is not all things and above all things. Now behold, if God were some thing, this or that, He would not be all in all, and above all, as He is; and so also, He would not be true perfection. Therefore God is, and yet He is neither this nor that which the creature, as creature, can perceive, name, conceive, or express. Therefore if God were this or that good, He would not be all good, and therefore He would not be the One Perfect Good, which He is. Now God is also a Light and a Reason . . . and inasmuch as God is Light and Reason, He must give light and perceive. Give heed to this. Behold! even as God is the one Good and Light and Reason, so is He also Will and Love and Justice and Truth, and in short all virtues.

PRAYER: *My God, my God, help me this day to know thy mind, and think thy thoughts, and manifest thy nature, and express thy life, and be a channel of thy love, and live as the agent and instrument of thy Spirit. In the name of Jesus Christ. Amen.*

12TH DAY

GOD AN INEXHAUSTIBLE OCEAN

I girded thee, though thou hast not known me.
ISAIAH 45:5

Read ISAIAH 45:5-7

In this life our perfection will consist in approaching as near as may be to contemplation of God without sensible forms, and as He is indeed proposed by faith, that is, not represented, but obscure notions imprinted in our minds concerning Him, by which we perceive that He is not anything that we can perceive or imagine, but an inexhaustible ocean of universal being and good, infinitely exceeding our comprehension; which being and good, whatsoever it is in itself, we love with the whole possible extension of our wills, embracing God beyond the proportion of our knowing Him.

PRAYER: *Thou, O God, who art able to do all things, renew my spirit, enlighten my understanding, sanctify my will, increase my strength of body and soul, that I may depend only on Thee, fear and love Thee above all things, and serve Thee fervently; and that in all my affections hereafter I may conform myself to thy blessed will and pleasure. In the name of Jesus Christ I pray. Amen.*

13TH DAY

WE MUST HAVE LIGHT

And God said, Let there be light: and there was light. GENESIS 1:3

Read MATTHEW 6:22-24

Often God penetrates my soul with a clarity, a joy so intense, that it seems as if the human frame could not bear them, and I would like to break out in cries of admiration at the vision of these interior spectacles. . . . This evening as my prayer was drawing to an end I had one of those spiritual *illumina-*

tions which are something unspeakable. Full sunlight suddenly flooding a dark prison would not give an idea of this illumination of the soul. In a flash of lightning all is changed, transfigured in her. It is God! What more can be said?

PRAYER: *O thou never-failing Light, Lord our God, the Fountain of Light, the Light of thine angels, principalities, powers, and of all intelligent beings, who hast created the light of thy saints, help me so that my soul shall be a lamp of thine, kindled and illuminated by Thee. Help me so that it shall shine and burn with the Truth, and never go out in darkness and ashes. Help me so that the gloom of all my sin shall be cleared away, and Light perpetual shall abide within me. Amen.*

14TH DAY

ALL THINGS FOR THE LOVE OF GOD

Whether therefore ye eat, or drink, or whatsoever ye do, do all to the glory of God.   I CORINTHIANS 10:31

Read EPHESIANS 5:15-21

We search for stated ways and methods of learning how to love God, and to come at that love we disquiet our minds by I know not how many devices; we give ourselves a world of trouble and pursue a multitude of practices to attain to a sense of the Presence of God. And yet it is so simple. How very much shorter it is and easier to do our *common business* purely *for the love of* God, to set his consecrating mark on all we lay our hands to, and thereby to foster the sense of his abiding Presence by communion of our *heart* with his!

PRAYER: *O thou Father of all mankind, help me to remember Thee in all I do and say, even in what seem to be the least of things. Let me not fail to remember at all times the world's need of a right knowledge of Thee; and help me therefore, in all my life, to bear true witness to Thee. And to Thee be the praise. Amen.*

15TH DAY

THE NEARNESS OF CHRIST

Lo, I am with you alway, even unto the end of the world.   MATTHEW 28:20

Read MATTHEW 28:16-20

All experience comes to be but more and more of pressure of His life on ours. It cannot come by one flash of light, or one great convulsive event. It comes without haste and without rest in the perpetual living of our life with Him. And all the history, of outer or inner life, of the changes of circumstances, or the changes of thought, gets its meaning and value from this constantly growing relation to Christ. I cannot tell you how personal this grows to me. He is here. He knows me and I know Him. It is no figure of speech. It is the realest thing in the world. And every day makes it realer. And one wonders with delight what it will grow to as the years go on.

PRAYER: *O Lord Christ, to think of Thee is to rest; to know Thee is eternal life; to see Thee is daily inspiration; to serve Thee is perfect freedom and the gate to everlasting joy. I desire to be thy true follower and companion, and I open my heart to thy continual indwelling. Amen.*

16TH DAY

MAN'S HIGH CAPACITY

The joy of the Lord is your strength.   NEHEMIAH 8:10

Read NEHEMIAH 8:1-10

The high capacity for delight in the God and Father of Jesus is in every soul. Then the lover of God becomes the host of God. We confess this truth in our prayer when we do pray; when we stop mere mumbling, when we lift ourselves out of conventions, when our whole nature rises to speak to God; we know then that communion with God means joy and that it is the very heart of existence. It is at this point that we discover the mournful poverty of our religious experience. How seldom we think of our heavenly Father as joy. How infrequently we lift our thought to the Eternal and sun ourselves in his supreme compassion! How infrequent our effort to live by his wisdom translated into our own thought, to go in the strength of his passionate and infinite love operating through our hearts, and to rest in the great power of his will.

PRAYER: *O Love of God, why do I seek Thee afar off when Thou art the life of my life and the love that yearneth in my heart? Whence these strange longings which prompt me to prayer, if it be not that Thou art moving behind my mind? Thou Infinite Nearness, amid all trials make me, by thy grace, to be a triumphant soul. Amen.*

17TH DAY

PEACE INSTEAD OF RESTLESSNESS

This kind can come forth by nothing, but by prayer.
MARK 9:29

Read MARK 9:14-29

Very gradually the practice of the presence of God, with its deep and silent communion, became an abiding joy to me as my heart was more at leisure from itself. Instead of the former restlessness, a new peace came flowing in. Far beyond all human words to express it, my one supreme joy was this, that the consciousness of Christ's own living presence was brought intimately near to me with a fullness of love that I had never known before. Just as I had felt a close companionship with Christ in the midst of human needs—among the poor and the needy, by the bedside of the sick and suffering, in the loneliness of the stranger, among the outcast and despised—so now I felt his presence in a new and living way through this deep peace which had flooded my whole being. What had been almost fugitive before became now more constant.

PRAYER: *Thou, O Lord, in every age didst send testimonies from heaven, and miracles of power and mercy; and, in the fulness of time, spakest to us by thy Son, who brought us to the knowledge of the true and only God our Father. Help me, I pray, to live this day, and every day, in consciousness of thy Presence, and to walk in companionship with Christ Jesus. In the name of thy Son. Amen.*

THE SOUL FEELS GOD PRESENT

Our God is a consuming fire.   HEBREWS 12:29

Read DEUTERONOMY 4:15-24

The first benefit which the soul receives from the Presence of God is that *faith grows more alive.* The soul, by a simple remembrance, feels God present, and calls upon Him freely and with assurance of response. Hope breathes into the will a distrust of things seen, and sets it aflame with the consuming fire of Divine love; for God's love is in very truth a consuming fire, burning to ashes all that is contrary to His will: the soul thus kindled cannot live save in the Presence of God, and this Presence works within the heart a consecrated zeal, a holy ardour. By the practice of the Presence of God, by steadfast *gaze* on Him, the soul comes to a knowledge of God, full and deep, to *an Unclouded Vision.*

PRAYER: *O Lord, help me, I pray, to realize at all times thy loving succor pledged to me, thy protecting Presence surrounding me, thy all-seeing eye fixed upon me, thy Divine heart yearning over me; and help me, therefore, not to go weakly and hesitatingly and falteringly through life, but steadfastly in thy strength. In the name of Jesus Christ. Amen.*

19TH DAY

GOD SO CLOSE

There came a cloud, and overshadowed them . . . and there came a voice out of the cloud. LUKE 9:34, 35

Read LUKE 9:28-36

Today God seems to me to be just behind everything. I feel Him there. He is just under my hand, just under the typewriter, just behind this desk, just inside the file, just inside the camera. That is how I feel about God today. Of course this is only a way of symbolizing the truth that God is invisible and that he is everywhere. I cannot imagine seeing the invisible, but I can imagine God hiding himself behind everything in sight. There is something infinitely comforting in feeling God so close, so *everywhere!* Nowhere one turns is away from friendship, for God is smiling there. It is difficult to convey to another the *joy* of having broken into the new sea of realizing God's "here-ness." When he gives himself he is giving more than anything else in the universe.

PRAYER: *Lord, I pray not for tranquillity, nor that my tribulations may cease. I pray that Thou wilt help me to live continually in the consciousness of thy Presence, thy Spirit, and thy Love. In the name of Jesus Christ, thy Son. Amen.*

20TH DAY

THE LORD IS IN THIS PLACE

Surely the Lord is in this place . . . this is none other but the house of God, and this is the gate of heaven.   GENESIS 28:16, 17

Read GENESIS 28:10-22

I am now venturing to give you the conviction, crystal clear in my consciousness, which I never can lose, which has come to me out of the discipline of mental pain and physical suffering. I have experienced an awareness of Christ, a certainty of his presence beside me and within me, a conviction that the age-old "mystic union" is true and possible today, to which I must give testimony so long as my life on earth endures. This is the form in which the experience came to me: Called upon suddenly to look squarely into the face of permanently crippled powers and the surrender of the work to which I had given myself for twenty years, I was upheld and sustained by my consciousness that Christ was intimately with me, giving me strength. I heard the promises of Jesus, I say, spoken to me in a hospital room. I heard him say, "Let not your heart be troubled." My Master and Lord told me not to fear. I did not and I do not. I heard him say, "Peace I leave with you." I was not saying over words for my consolation. Christ was speaking. And peace became mine. Perhaps the tides may ebb and flow; but I know that I shall never lose it wholly.

PRAYER: *My God! my God! Thou art with me here and now. Help me to realize thy Presence. Amen.*

21ST DAY

DEATH A GLORIOUS ADVENTURE

The river of God . . . is full of water.   PSALM 65:9

Read PSALM 65

I heard him say, "Because I live, ye shall live also." And so I knew beyond a doubt; *death cannot stop me.* There were no speculative questions; there were no doubts. I knew that I should go on; that I would still be I. Now I look forward to the episode of physical death as a glorious adventure. I have no more fear of meeting it than I could have had in the old college days when I went home to my father's house and the room prepared for me by my mother's love. I have even anticipated what I yearn to do in the Father's vast house of being. Now I know what Paul meant when he said that Christ breaks the bonds of those in slavery through their fear of death. Thus he brought me the living conviction of the reality and power of the life immortal.

PRAYER: *Essence beyond essence, Nature increate, Framer of the world, I set Thee, Lord, before my face, and I lift up my soul unto Thee. I stretch forth my hands unto Thee, my soul is as a thirsty land towards Thee. Thou, O Lord, I beseech Thee, in thine unspeakable love, so order concerning me, and so dispose, as Thou knowest to be most pleasing to Thee, and most good for me. Amen.*

THE FIRST IMPERATIVE

Thou shalt love the Lord thy God with all thy heart, and with all thy soul, and with all thy mind, and with all thy strength.   MARK 12:30

Read MARK 12:28-34

Not with doubting, but with assured consciousness, do I love Thee, Lord. But what do I love, when I love Thee? not beauty of bodies, nor the fair harmony of time, nor the brightness of the light, so gladsome to our eyes, nor sweet melodies of varied songs, nor the fragrant smell of flowers, and ointments, and spices, not manna and honey, not limbs acceptable to embracements of flesh. None of these I love, when I love my God; and yet I love a kind of light, and melody, and fragrance, and meat, and embracement, when I love my God, the light, melody, fragrance, meat, embracement of my inner man: where there shineth unto my soul, what space cannot contain, and there soundeth, what time beareth not away, and there smelleth, what breathing disperseth not, and there tasteth, what eating diminisheth not, and there clingeth, what satiety divorceth not. This is it which I love, when I love my God.

PRAYER: *O God of love, whose love is ever round about thy children, increase in me that love of Thee which will keep my soul lifted up into the realm where thy spirit dwells. Glory be to Thee, O Lord. Amen.*

23RD DAY

TO MAKE THE SOUL EFFECTIVE

Let us not love in word, neither in tongue; but in deed and in truth.   1 JOHN 3:18

Read 1 JOHN 3:13-20

The true proficiency of the soul consists not so much in deep thinking or eloquent speaking or beautiful writing as in much and warm loving. Now if you ask me what way this much warm love may be acquired, I answer—by resolving to do the will

22

of God, and by watching to do his will as often as occasion offers. Those who truly love God love all good wherever they find it. They seek all good to all men. They encourage all good to all men. They commend all good, they always unite themselves with all good, they always acknowledge and defend all good. O Lord, give me more and more of this blessed love.

PRAYER: *O God, I who have loved too few, and none aright, beseech Thee to teach me how to love. Show me the hungry hearts of men and women. To all weakness which men bear as a burden from the past, make me merciful; to all moral defeat make me forgiving, even as I crave forgiveness for my-self. Help me to look upon the struggling and thwarted souls of men with insight and sympathy. Melt my hardness, O Lord, and lift my life into thy fellowship that true love may live in me. Amen.*

24TH DAY

RECOLLECTION ANYWHERE

Beloved, building up yourselves on your most holy faith, praying in the Holy Ghost, keep yourselves in the love of God.   JUDE 20, 21

Read JUDE 20-25

I was present at a musical party and . . . I be-sought the Beloved to repose still in my heart where I wished to make a perpetual feast for Him. I adored

Him there and recommended to Him all those who were present, especially those souls who seemed to me most exposed to danger and those, alas, whose falls are only too well known and too certain. Our Lord filled my soul with his presence which dominated all exterior impressions. How great and tender appeared Jesus to me and how above and beyond our trivial daily occupations.

PRAYER: *How truly meet, and right, and comely, and due, in all, and for all, in all times, places, manners, in every season, every spot, everywhere, always, altogether, to remember Thee, to worship Thee, to confess to Thee, to praise Thee, to bless Thee, to hymn Thee, to give thanks to Thee, Lord and Father, King and God, Fountain of life and immortality: full is the whole heaven, and the whole earth, of the majesty of thy glory. Amen.*

25TH DAY

LIFE'S TURNING POINT

And suddenly there shined round about him a light from heaven. ACTS 9:3

Read ACTS 9:1-16

After Francis had returned to Assisi—and not many days after—on a certain evening he was chosen by his companions as master of their revels. . . . He accordingly then caused a rich feast to be prepared, as he had done many times before. When they had regaled themselves, they went forth from the house . . . singing as they went through the city, he himself carrying in his hand a wand as their master. And lo! suddenly he was visited by the Lord, and with so much sweetness was his heart filled, that he was able neither to speak nor to move. But when his companions looked behind and saw him far away from them, turning back towards him, they in their fear took him to be as it were changed already into another man. And they questioned him: "Why hast thou not come up to us? Perchance thou hast been thinking of taking to thyself a wife!" He with a loud voice replied to them: "Ye have spoken truly, since I have been thinking of taking to myself a spouse nobler, richer, and more beautiful than ever [I] have seen." . . . That spouse was true religion.

PRAYER: *Let me also receive light from Thee, O my God—the light I need. Amen.*

26TH DAY

PEACE BECAUSE OF FAITH

Thy faith hath saved thee; go in peace.   LUKE 7:50

Read LUKE 7:36-50

As for the faults which are not noticed until after they have been committed, the fretting and vexation of self-love never mends them. On the contrary, this vexation is only an impatience of pride at the

25

sight of what mortifies it. The only thing to do with our faults, then, is to humiliate ourselves on their account in peace. I say in Peace, because it is not being humiliated, if we take our humiliation with chagrin and reluctance. We must condemn our fault, without seeking its softening by any excuse, and see ourselves before God without confusion, without being bitter against ourselves and without being discouraged, but profiting quietly by the humiliation of our fault. The confusion of sin, when it is received in a soul which does not bear it impatiently, is the remedy for sin itself. But it is not being humble, to resist humiliation.

PRAYER: *O Lord, my Lord, give me grace to lay aside every weight, and the sin which doth so easily beset me, and every motion of flesh and spirit alienated from the will of thy holiness; and help me so to hunger and thirst after righteousness that I be filled. In the name of Jesus Christ. Amen.*

27TH DAY

BE OPEN TO LIGHT CONTINUALLY

The light of the body is the eye: if therefore thine eye be single, thy whole body shall be full of light. MATTHEW 6:22

Read MATTHEW 6:22-24

This morning, when I sat down to meditate, I felt

26

full of inward light, a lovely interior sunshine. As one knows the feeling of the sun pouring over one from without, so this was the shining of a sun within. I saw that the present enterprise for me was to make this inner light penetrate further and further into each day's ordinary activity. From half-past nine until ten this morning I was in heaven. I am sure that through persistent effort and the gradual removal of obstacles, it is possible to make the light shine through more and more hours of the day, until finally the kingdom comes upon one's earth not alone from half-past nine to ten, but for every minute of one's existence.

PRAYER: *O my God, in whom I live, and move, and have my being, let my spirit meet and mingle with thy Spirit at this moment, and let me receive thy Light inwardly all through this day. In the name of Jesus Christ. Amen.*

28TH DAY

FINDING THE LIGHT UNCHANGEABLE

God is light, and in him is no darkness at all.
1 JOHN 1:5

Read 1 JOHN 1:5-10

And being thence admonished to return to myself, I entered even into my inward self, Thou being my

Guide: and able I was, for Thou wert become my Helper. And I entered and beheld with the eye of my soul, (such as it was,) above the same eye of my soul, above my mind, the Light Unchangeable. Not this ordinary light, which all flesh may look upon, nor as it were a greater of the same kind, as though the brightness of this should be manifold brighter, and with its greatness take up all space. Not such was this light, but other, yea, far other from all these. Nor was it above my soul, as oil is above water, nor yet as heaven above earth: but above to my soul, because It made me; and I below It, because I was made by It. He that knows the Truth, knows what that Light is; and he that knows It, knows eternity. Love knoweth It. O Truth who art Eternity! and Love who art Truth! and Eternity who art Love! Thou art my God, to Thee do I sigh night and day.

PRAYER: *Help me, O Thou who art Light Unchangeable, to see myself by thy Light and to change myself as I need to be changed, and thus to grow unto the perfect man, unto the measure of the stature of the fullness of Christ. Amen.*

NOT CONFORMED, BUT TRANSFORMED

Be not conformed to this world: but be ye transformed by the renewing of your mind. ROMANS 12:2

Read ROMANS 12:1-21

I want to live, I want to live, if God will give me help, such a life that, if all the men in the world were living it, this world would be regenerated and saved. I want to live such a life that, if that life changed into new personal peculiarities as it went to different men, but the same life still, if every man were living it, the millennium would be here; nay, heaven would be here, the universal presence of God.

PRAYER: *Infinite Father, teach me how great a faith I have inherited respecting the Ultimate Reality of the mysterious universe in which I am living, the faith that God is love, the faith that God is light and in Him is no darkness at all. Teach me, my Father, how great a Master and Leader I have in my Lord Jesus who went about declaring that He was the Light of the world and that whosoever followeth Him shall not walk in darkness but shall have the light of life. Help me to hear the great call for myself to come out of all waste and desecration of my power, and to let my light so shine before men that they may see my good works and glorify my Father who is in Heaven. And to Thee be glory forevermore. Amen.*

THE MARKS OF JESUS

I bear in my body the marks of the Lord Jesus.
GALATIANS 6:17

Read GALATIANS 6:14-18

As the seraph swiftly drew nigh, Saint Francis saw that he bore the image of a man crucified. And it was revealed to him that not by the sufferings of the body but by the burning enthusiasm of the soul, would he be transformed into the express image of Christ Crucified in that marvellous celestial presentation. . . . After a long and mysterious commune with his Divine Lord there was left in the heart of Saint Francis an overpowering fire of Divine love, and on his body there was impressed a wondrous semblance and image of the passion of Christ. Upon his hands and feet there began straightway to appear the marks of the nails, as he had seen them on the body of the Crucified Jesus Christ, in the seraphic apparition; and on his right side there appeared the resemblance of a still open wound, as though made by a lance.

PRAYER: *O my God, I want the marks of the Lord Jesus to be manifest in me—his character, his wisdom, his compassion, his creative love, his sacrifice of self, his loveliness. Help me, I pray. And to Him be praise forevermore. Amen.*

WE ARE TO BE LIKE HIM

Beloved, now are we the sons of God, and it doth not yet appear what we shall be. We know that, when he shall appear, we shall be like him: for we shall see him as he is.   1 JOHN 3:2

Read 1 JOHN 3:1-3

A philosopher says, God hawks Himself to all creatures and each takes as much as it wants. I trow God offers Himself to me as he does to the highest angel and were I as apt as He is I should receive as he does. . . . He alone is the Lord and the spirit. I say, He is spirit; our happiness lies in union with Him. . . . Lo, He is Lord and spirit, may He beatify us by uniting us with Him.

PRAYER: *Infinite Father, I thank Thee for my personal experience of Thee, and for the truths that come to me from that experience. Accept my thanksgiving, and grant me insight increasingly, and courage to live up to my insights; strengthen my will for service, and make the life that I live here and now a moral victory, a joy, an unconquerable hope, and a foretaste of the perfection that is yet to be. In the name of Jesus Christ. Amen.*

WE MUST HAVE CHRIST IN US

Christ in you, the hope of glory.   COLOSSIANS 1:27

Read COLOSSIANS 1:23-29

As marriage between man and wife is binding, so there is eternal marriage between your souls and God. A maid is given to a man hoping to bear his child. And God did make the soul intending her to bear in her his one-begotten Son. The happening of this birth in Mary ghostly was to God better pleasing than his being born of her in flesh. And this same birth today in the God-loving soul delights God more than his creation of the heavens and earth.

It is more worth to God his being brought forth ghostly in the individual virgin or good soul than that He was born of Mary bodily.

PRAYER: *O Christ Spirit, Spirit that was in Jesus, be in me continually. Help me so that I also shall live this life among men as a true child of God, offering to the world through my words and acts at all times his mind and love and salvation. And to Him be praise forever. Amen.*

THE PRACTICE OF
GOD'S PRESENCE

My soul, wait thou only upon God.   PSALM 62:5

Read PSALM 62:5-8

I cannot imagine how religious persons can live satisfied without the practice of *the presence of* God. For my part, I keep myself retired with Him in the fund or centre of my soul as much as I can; and while I am so with Him I fear nothing, but the least turning from Him is insupportable. I do not say that therefore we must put any violent constraint upon ourselves. No, we must serve God in a holy freedom; we must do our business faithfully; without trouble or disquiet, recalling our mind to God mildly, and with tranquility, as often as we find it wandering from Him. Accustom yourself, then, by degrees, thus to worship Him, to beg his grace, to offer Him your heart from time to time in the midst of your business, even every moment, if you can. Do not always scrupulously confine yourself to certain rules, or particular forms of devotion, but act with a general confidence in God, with love and humility.

PRAYER: *O thou Infinite and Eternal, our Father in heaven, help me to live in awareness of Thee as I do my work this day. Let thy still, small voice whisper within me, so that I shall be continually taught, guided, and inspired by Thee, and made more ready to live up to the opportunities the day affords. And to Thee be the praise and glory. Amen.*

34TH DAY

SIMPLE ATTENTION

I will bless the Lord at all times: his praise shall continually be in my mouth.   PSALM 34:1

Read PSALM 34

I have quitted all forms of devotion and set prayers but those to which my state obliges me. And I make it my business only to persevere in His holy presence, wherein I keep myself by a simple attention, and a general fond regard to God, which I may call an *actual presence* of God; or, to speak better, an habitual, silent and secret conversation of the soul with God, which often causes me joys and raptures inwardly, and sometimes also outwardly, so great, that I am forced to use means to moderate them and prevent their appearance to others.

PRAYER: *O Infinite Love, the Source, the Way, the Goal of all true life: help me to feel the tides of thy Being sweeping round my being. Help me to open the flood-gates of my life to the ocean of thy life. And help me to catch sight of that immortal sea which brought me hither, and upon which I shall sail forth again. In the name of Jesus Christ. Amen.*

SIMPLICITY IN PRAYER

Be it unto thee even as thou wilt.   MATTHEW 15:28

Read MATTHEW 15:22-28

I find it usually easier to pray for others than for myself. I believe in beginning by praying for what is easiest. I don't kneel down. I find it more possible to concentrate my attention when I am walking about or sitting down. And I tell God what I know about a man, and how I want him to live a better life. I go on and on and on—sometimes repeating the same request. I try to copy the poor widow who wearied out the dishonest judge. I am not distressed when my thoughts wander. The distress occasioned by wandering thoughts, and the attempt to trace the stages by which they wandered, I regard as temptations of the devil. I go back as calmly as possible to the matter in hand. Don't think too much about yourself when you pray. You must lose your soul if you would save it.

PRAYER: *O Lord God Almighty, Father of the Lord Jesus Christ, of whom the whole family in heaven and earth is named, strengthen me, I pray, by thy Spirit in the inner man, and fill me with the fullness of that Christ who worked for the physically suffering and spiritually blind and weak, so that I may carry on his work in the world. Amen.*

SEEK GOD FOR HIMSELF

Fear God, and give glory to him . . . and worship him that made heaven, and earth, and the sea, and the fountains of waters.   REVELATION 14:7

Read ACTS 8:9-24

Meister Eckhart asks, Whose are the prayers God always hears? And Meister Eckhart answers, Who worships God as God, God hears. But he who worships God for worldly goods, worships not God: he worships what he worships God for, and employs God as his servant for the getting of it.

PRAYER: *Blesséd, and praised, and celebrated, and magnified, and exalted, and glorified, and hallowed, be thy name, O Lord, its record, and its memory, and every memorial of it. Amen.*

WIN BY ACQUIESCENCE

But I say unto you, That ye resist not evil: but whosoever shall smite thee on thy right cheek, turn to him the other also.   MATTHEW 5:39

Read MATTHEW 5:38-42

Our Lord encouraged me . . . not only to preserve my peace, but also suavity of soul, in the midst of

those sufferings which come from our fellow-creatures, and He gave me these means ... to speak to
them with a particular and very marked kindness;
to avoid the slightest allusion to the wrongs they
have done me when it is not absolutely necessary
to do so; in short, to take care that in all circumstances, whenever I speak of them, my words should
be full of charity. So be it, my Lord! It is sweet to
work after such a model as Thee! Yes, to-day, in this
very moment, when cares and contradictions give
me no truce, yes, for Thy sake, I can love that which
is not lovable, remain silent when all my blood is
boiling, act according to duty without any proba-
bility of meeting approval, pray and offer my soul
for those who torment her. Yes, for Thee, one can,
one ought, to do all this, and the soul may, by a
special grace of thine, forget all things and ascend
to Thee.

PRAYER: *O Thou through whom alone can I have
true life, take hold upon me and within me, with
thy might mightily, and give me the strength I
need. In the name of Jesus Christ. Amen.*

HOW ACHIEVE FRIENDSHIP
WITH GOD?

As the body without the spirit is dead, so faith without works is dead also.   JAMES 2:26

Read JAMES 2:14-26

Knowing God better and better is an achievement of friendship. How is it to be achieved? By doing things together. The depth and intensity of the friendship will depend upon the variety and extent of the things we do and enjoy together. . . . All I have said is mere words, until one sets out helping God right wrongs, helping God help the helpless, loving and talking it over with God. Then there comes a great sense of the close up, warm intimate heart of reality. God simply creeps in and you *know* he is here in your heart.

PRAYER: *The power of the Father guide me, the wisdom of the Son enlighten me, the working of the Spirit quicken me. Guard Thou my soul, strengthen my body, direct my course, order my habits, shape my character, inspire holy thoughts, pardon the past, correct the present, prevent the future. And to Thee, my God, be glory. Amen.*

FLUCTUATION

Why art thou cast down, O my soul? hope thou in God: for I shall yet praise him.   PSALM 42:11

Read PSALM 42

After this conversion, which so altered my whole life, I was for a period of some months in such a state of exaltation and enhancement of all my faculties that I did not know myself at all. The most beautiful music flowed through my mind. Colour and form, imagery of all kinds, would pass through me till I felt like an artist. An object of quite ordinary charm seemed, because of that something which now filled me, to expand into prodigious beauty! The world was turned into a veritable paradise! But this wonderful state of things gradually passed away. At one time of the day I would be in an ecstasy of delight, and an hour later in some altogether unreasonable depth of wretchedness. I prayed for two things—that I might love God with a cheerful countenance, and that He would teach me quickly what to pray for. Next, I banished my own feelings as much as I could, concerning myself at all times of the day to loving inward conversation with [Jesus]; and in this manner I fastened myself closer than ever to Him.

PRAYER: *O Thou in whom I live, and move, and have my being, help me to live in realization of thy ever-nearness. In the name of Jesus Christ. Amen.*

FROM VISIBLE TO INVISIBLE

And the children of Israel saw the face of Moses, that the skin of Moses' face shone: and Moses put the veil upon his face again, until he went in to speak with him.   EXODUS 34:35

Read EXODUS 34:29-35

How is it that we can pass so, up from the visible into the Invisible, and become so oned with it, and feel it so powerfully, that the Invisible becomes a thousand times more real to us than the visible! We may wonder how it is that the Mighty Maker of the Universe should choose to condescend to the mere individual piece of clay. It is incomprehensible. It is so incomprehensible that there is but one way of looking at it. This is no favouritism to the individual, but the evidence of a Mind with a vast plan pursuing a way and using a likely individual. These individuals or willing souls He takes and fashions them to His own ends and liking. Of one He will make a worker, and of another He fashions to Himself a lover. It would seem to be His will to use the human implement to help the human.

PRAYER: *O Thou eternal Creator, fashion me, I pray, to do in the world the work Thou wouldst have me do for Thee. In the name of Jesus Christ. Amen.*

KNOW GOD IN VERY TRUTH

This is thankworthy, if a man for conscience toward God endure grief, suffering wrongfully. I PETER 2:19

Read I PETER 2:13-25

Before all things it is necessary that [man] should know God in very truth, and not only outwardly and superficially; he must understand His supreme worthiness, His supreme beauty, sweetness, exaltedness, virtue, goodness, liberality, mercy, and pity, and he must understand that God is the supreme good and highest of all; and He, who is supremely good, giveth Himself unto the lover. Then doth the soul participate in that supreme good, which is supreme love. Then, by the virtue of love, is the lover transformed in the beloved and the beloved is transformed in the lover, and like unto hard iron which so assumeth the colour, heat, virtue, and form of the fire that it almost turneth into fire, so doth the soul, united with God through the perfect grace of divine love, itself almost become divine. Its whole life is transformed in the love of God.

PRAYER: *Transform me, O my God! Transform me from what I am into what I ought to be. Amen.*

THE EXPERIENCE OF GOD

For every one that asketh receiveth; and he that seeketh findeth; and to him that knocketh it shall be opened.   MATTHEW 7:8

Read MATTHEW 7:7-12

Its rapture [the rapture of the experience of God] is not swooning but an intense adoration and a thrilling vitality. It is possession, ardent, demonic, divine, when the whole self is gripped and energised and controlled by a power whose influence leaves no room for self-consciousness or self-regard or any single disharmony of impulse. It is in this experience when wholeness of personal life is seized upon by a transcending and irresistible power, a power other than the self, yet akin to it and able to possess and use it, that the true mysticism consists. In it is no abdication of consciousness, but its consummation; no passivity, but an intense and dynamic energy; no enfolding Comforter, but Deity, creative, redemptive, unresting in movement, unchanging in purpose, a majesty beside which the placid heaven of the Contemplative fades into a dream, a splendour which takes up suffering into itself and transfigures it.

PRAYER: *O my God, take my mind and think through it. Take my lips and speak through them. Take my heart and set it on fire with love for Thee. In the name of Jesus Christ. Amen.*

LIVING WITH GOD EVERYWHERE

And he said unto him, Lord, thou knowest all things; thou knowest that I love thee. Jesus saith unto him, Feed my sheep.   JOHN 21:17

Read JOHN 21:15-22

To a hermit who had scruples about changing from a life of solitude and worship to a life of active service out in the needy world, Saint Catherine of Siena wrote: "Now the hour is come that proves who is a servant of God, and whether men shall seek themselves for their own sake, and God for the private consolation they find in Him, and whether we are to believe that God may be found only in one place and not in another. I do not see that this is so—but find that to the true servant of God every place is the right place and every time is the right time. So when the time comes to abandon his own consolations and embrace labours for the honour of God, he does it; and when the time comes to flee the wood for need of the honour of God, he does it, and betakes him to public places. Now really, the spiritual life is quite too lightly held if it is lost by change of place."

PRAYER: *My God! my God! I give myself utterly to Thee to be shaped by Thee, led by Thee, placed by Thee, and used by Thee as Thou wilt and where Thou wilt, as the agent and instrument of thy Spirit. Amen.*

PARTAKING OF THE DIVINE NATURE

Whereby are given unto us exceeding great and precious promises: that by these ye might be partakers of the divine nature.   II PETER 1:4

Read II PETER 1:1-8

I am sure there is a common Spirit that plays within us, yet makes no part of us; and that is, the Spirit of God, the fire and scintillation of that noble and mighty Essence, which is the life and radical heat of Spirits, and those essences that know not the vertue of the Sun. This is that gentle heat that brooded on the waters, and in six days hatched the World; this is that irradiation that dispels the mists of Hell, the clouds of horrour, fear, sorrow, despair; and preserves the region of the mind in serenity. Whosoever feels not the warm gale and gentle ventilation of this Spirit, though I feel his pulse, I dare not say he lives: for truely, without this, to me there is no heat under the Tropick; nor any light, though I dwelt in the body of the Sun.

PRAYER: *O my God, fill me, body, mind, heart, and soul, with the Spirit that was in Jesus. I give unto Thee my thinking, talking, and acting that Thou mayest shape me in the likeness of Christ, and direct me through thy everlasting love and to thy praise. Amen.*

THE SPIRITUAL IS THE REAL

But the manifestation of the Spirit is given to every man to profit withal.   I CORINTHIANS 12:7

Read I CORINTHIANS 12:1-11

"Yes, it is true that there are moments when the flesh is nothing to me, when I feel and know the flesh to be the vision, God and the Spiritual the only real and true. Depend upon it, the Spiritual *is* the real: it belongs to one more than the hand and the foot. You may tell me that my hand and my foot are only imaginary symbols of my existence, I could believe you; but you never, never can convince me that the *I* is not an eternal Reality, and that the Spiritual is not the true and real part of me." These words he [Tennyson] spoke with such passionate earnestness that a solemn silence fell on us as he left the room.

PRAYER: *O Light of light, enlighten my soul, sanctify my body, govern my affections, and guide my thoughts, that in the fastest closure of my eyelids my spirit may see Thee. Suffer me not, O my God, to forget Thee either in the darkness or in the light. In the name of Jesus Christ, thy interpreter. Amen.*

SPIRIT WITH SPIRIT CAN MEET

And Jesus, when he was baptized, went up straightway out of the water: and, lo, the heavens were opened unto him, and he saw the Spirit of God descending like a dove, and lighting upon him.
MATTHEW 3:16

Read MATTHEW 3:13-17

A kind of waking trance I [Tennyson] have frequently had, quite up from boyhood, when I have been all alone. This has generally come upon me thro' repeating my own name two or three times to myself silently, till all at once, as it were out of the intensity of the consciousness of individuality, the individuality itself seemed to dissolve and fade away into boundless being, and this not a confused state, but the clearest of the clearest, the surest of the surest, the weirdest of the weirdest, where death was an almost laughable impossibility, the loss of personality (if so it were) seeming no extinction but the only true life. This might be the state which St. Paul describes, "Whether in the body I cannot tell, or whether out of the body I cannot tell."

PRAYER: *O Lord, my God, unseen but as near as the life within my own body, help me to live in continual communion with Thee. Let my spirit meet and mingle with thy Spirit, my mind with thy Mind, my heart with thy Heart, my life with thy Life. In the name of Jesus Christ, thy Son. Amen.*

PEACE AT ALL TIMES

The peace of God, which passeth all understanding, shall keep your hearts and minds through Christ Jesus.   PHILIPPIANS 4:7

Read PHILIPPIANS 4:4-7

But you will find in all that happens to you, all that opposes and grieves you—even in those inevitable hours of darkness when the doors of true perception seem to close, and the cruel tangles of the world are all that you can discern—an inward sense of security which will never cease. All the waves that buffet you about, shaking sometimes the strongest faith and hope, are yet parts and aspects of one Ocean. Did they wreck you utterly, that Ocean would receive you; and there you would find, overwhelming and transforming you, the unfathomable Substance of all life and joy.

PRAYER: *O God of peace, who hast taught us that in returning and rest we shall be saved, that in quietness and confidence shall be our strength; by the might of thy Holy Spirit lift me, I pray, to thy Presence, that I may be still and know that Thou art God at all times and under all conditions: through Jesus Christ our Lord. Amen.*

SILENT COMMUNING

Looking unto Jesus the author and finisher of our faith. HEBREWS 12:2

Read HEBREWS 12:1-3

Each evening, on his way home from work, an old French laborer used to stop at the parish church, put down his tools by the door, enter the hallowed place, and then kneel for a long while before the figure of Christ. One evening the curé stopped him as he was preparing to depart after his period of devotion, and asked: "What do you say to our Lord in these long visits that you pay Him?" The man replied: "I don't say anything to Him; I look up at Him, and He looks down at me."

PRAYER: *Lord Christ, my Savior, unto Thee I lift up my heart and my spirit. Help me to find the relief that I need from restlessness and anxiety, and to live in that power and peace which come from companionship with Thee. In all perplexity and distress help me to follow thy example of quiet confidence, and to walk in the strength of thy companionship. And to Thee be praise forevermore. Amen.*

AT ONE WITH GOD'S WILL

For we which live are alway delivered unto death for Jesus' sake, that the life also of Jesus might be made manifest in our mortal flesh.   II CORINTHIANS 4:11

Read II CORINTHIANS 4:7-11

What is this union? It is that we should be of a truth purely, simply, and wholly at one with the One Eternal Will of God, or altogether without will, so that the created will should flow out into the Eternal Will, and be swallowed up and lost therein. Now, when this union truly cometh to pass and becometh established, the inward man standeth henceforward immoveable in this union. So that the outward man saith in sincerity "I have no will to be or not to be, to live or die, to know or not to know, to do or to leave undone and the like; but I am ready for all that is to be, or ought to be, and obedient thereunto, whether I have to do or to suffer." And thus the outward man hath no Wherefore or purpose, but only to do his part to further the Eternal Will.

PRAYER: *Spirit of God, Spirit of light and truth, guide me, and guide my affairs, all through this day and continually, in all things perfectly. To the glory of God and of Christ Jesus, his Son. Amen.*

WE MUST KEEP IN TUNE

I do nothing of myself; but as my Father hath taught me.   JOHN 8:28

Read JOHN 8:12-30

A disciple came to Lu Chu in a state of self-satisfaction because he thought he had found the Way. Lu Chu perceived that his thinking was superficial, and that he must be helped to a deeper understanding of what the right living of life calls for. He therefore took two lutes, tuned them to the same pitch, and placed one in the hall and one in the room adjoining it. Then when he struck the *kung* note on the one in the hall, the one in the next room answered with that same *kung* tone. Likewise when he sounded the *chio* note on the one, the *chio* note on the other made response. If, however, he changed the pitch of one of the strings of the lute in the hall the other instrument answered with only a jangle. The lesson was that it is necessary for a man to keep himself in tune with the Master Spirit of the universe. If he does that "its unspeakable power possesses him—he reacts to all its processes" and becomes a "channel of the Universal."

PRAYER: *Spirit of God, eternal Spirit, make use of me as Thou wilt, only help me to keep in tune with Thee at all times. Let no tie ever be broken which binds me to thy spirit, and thy mind, and thy service. In the name of Jesus Christ. Amen.*

THE INWARD MEETING-PLACE

Thou shalt rear up the tabernacle . . . where I will meet with you, to speak there unto thee.   EXODUS 26:30; 29:42

Read EXODUS 29:42-46

Deep within us all there is an amazing inner sanctuary of the soul, a holy place, a Divine Center, a speaking Voice, to which we may continuously return. Eternity is at our hearts, pressing upon our time-worn lives, warming us with intimations of an astounding destiny, calling us home unto Itself. Yielding to these persuasions, gladly committing ourselves in body and soul, utterly and completely, to the Light Within, is the beginning of true life. It is a dynamic center, a creative Life that presses to birth within us. It is a Light Within which illumines the face of God and casts new shadows and new glories upon the face of men. It is the Shekinah of the soul, the Presence in the midst.

PRAYER: *Infinite Father, Thou art my Maker and Thou art my sovereign and unchanging Friend, and I thank Thee that there is a place within me where I can meet Thee as the one who helps me to right understanding of my being, of my place in the world, of my frailties, of my sins, of my need for struggling, and of the hopes I can have because of Thee. Help me to perceive and fulfill thy purpose concerning me. In the name of Jesus Christ. Amen.*

A GOD WHO IS PERSONAL

Thus saith the Lord that created thee . . . thou art mine. ISAIAH 43:1

Read ISAIAH 43:1-5

I have more and more come to the conclusion for some time past that the only reality underlying and explaining the world must be personal. I know that I am a person, and that it is persons—especially a few particular persons—not things, who have influenced me and had a power in my life. All my ideas of justice and purity and goodness are inseparably bound up with persons. At last I have come to the conclusion that nothing exists except the personal, and that below all is One who is personal. That means to say that the world and things in it are only real in so far as they are thoughts of God. We are real only in so far as we are thoughts of God. . . . For life is a circle whose centre is God. . . . To die is to get a step nearer the centre. The closer we are connected with the centre, the nearer we are to those whom we call dead.

PRAYER: *Dispel, O Lord my God, the clouds of doubt and darkness from my mind, and help me in thy light to see light, and come both to know Thee as I am known, and to love Thee as I am loved. In the name of Jesus Christ. Amen.*

CONTACT WITH THE BEYOND

The word is very nigh unto thee.   DEUTERONOMY
30:14

Read DEUTERONOMY 30:11-14

When I get quite quiet, and my mind is sane, and
my conscience at rest, when I almost stop thinking,
and listen, I am quite sure that a Personal Being
comes to me, and, as He comes, brings some of his
own life to flow into my life. I am also sure that
with Him come those who live in Him, that all
whom I have known or know, and longed or long
to know better, who were *worth* knowing, are near
to me, are, if I let them, living their lives in my
life, making me what I should not be without them.
. . . What I have written is not a mere philosophy
of life; it is the only thing that makes life tolerable
for a moment to me. . . . So we are led on to Him
in whose image we are made, and whose image we
never so clearly reflect as when we love most.

PRAYER: *Enlighten, O Lord, my mind and heart
with thy Spirit, so that I may be continually aware
of Thee, and may live at all times in contact with
Thee, and with all the help that can come to me
from that Beyond in which Thou livest and in which
live all good spirits. In the name of Jesus Christ.
Amen.*

PRACTICE THE SOLID VIRTUES

The kingdom of heaven is like unto treasure hid in a field.   MATTHEW 13:44

Read MATTHEW 13:44-46

They shall not fail of salvation who practise themselves in the solid virtues. . . . Their Lord deals with them as with strong and valiant men, appointing them travail and trouble here, that they may fight for Him the good fight of faith, and only come in for the prize at the end. And, after all, what greater mark of a high election can there be than to taste much of the cross? Whom the Lord loveth, in that measure He lays on them His cross. And the heaviest of all our crosses is a life of sanctification and service without sensible consolation. . . . In short, let his Majesty lead us in any way He pleases. . . . God leads his people in the way that He chooses out as best for Him and for them. And he who stands low in his own eyes, may all the time stand high in God's eyes.

PRAYER: *O Lord, my God, who didst send to mankind a Light to lighten every soul coming into the world, help me to live each day in thy light, thy life, thy joy, and thy peace, and to do my work as the business of the Everlasting Father, and as being a worker together with Him. In the name of Jesus Christ. Amen.*

LIVING ON TWO LEVELS

Know ye not that ye are the temple of God, and that the Spirit of God dwelleth in you?   I CORINTHIANS 3:16

Read I CORINTHIANS 3:10-17

There is a way of ordering our mental life on more than one level at once. On one level we may be thinking, discussing, seeing, calculating, meeting all the demands of external affairs. But deep within, behind the scenes, at a profounder level, we may also be in prayer and adoration, song and worship and a gentle receptiveness to divine breathings. In a deeply religious culture men know that the deep level of prayer and of divine attendance is the most important thing in the world. It is at this deep level that the real business of life is determined. The religious mind involves the whole of man, embraces his relations with time within their true ground and setting in the Eternal Lover.

PRAYER: *O my God, I give myself to Thee, to live with Thee today in awareness of Thee, communion with Thee, union with Thee, quick and sure responsiveness to Thee. I take to myself thy Spirit and thy thoughts, I take the strength and the life that I need. Amen.*

THE SPIRIT OF PRAYER
CONTINUALLY

Rejoice evermore. Pray without ceasing. I THES-
SALONIANS 5:16, 17

Read 1 THESSALONIANS 5:12-24

How, then, shall we lay hold of that Life and
Power, and live the life of prayer without ceasing?
By quiet, persistent practice in turning of all our
being, day and night, in prayer and inward worship and surrender, toward Him who calls in the
deeps of our souls. Mental habits of inward orientation must be established. . . . In secret ejaculations
of praise, turn in humble wonder to the Light, faint
though it may be. Keep contact with the outer world
of sense and meanings. Here is no discipline in
absent-mindedness. Walk and talk and work and
laugh with your friends. But behind the scenes,
keep up the life of simple prayer and inward worship. Keep it up throughout the day. Let inward
prayer be your last act before you fall asleep and the
first act when you awake. And in time you will find
as did Brother Lawrence that "those who have the
gale of the Holy Spirit go forward even in sleep."

PRAYER: *O Thou whom I need more than all
else in the world, help me to order my mind and
soul in such wise that I shall live with Thee a life
of unceasing communion, loving the things which
Thou shalt command, and desiring those things*

which shall lead me continually into more light. In the name of Jesus Christ. Amen.

THE GREAT CONVICTION

It is a faithful saying: For if we be dead with him, we shall also live with him.   II TIMOTHY 2:11

Read II TIMOTHY 2:1-13

I can hardly understand how any great, imaginative man, who has deeply lived, suffered, thought and wrought, can doubt of the Soul's continuous progress in the after-life. . . . Is all this trouble of life worth undergoing if we only end in our own corpse-coffins at last? If you allow a God, and God allows this strong instinct and universal yearning for another life, surely that is in a measure a presumption of the truth. We cannot give up the mighty hopes that make us men.

PRAYER: *O Thou Infinite and Eternal, in thy love everlasting and thy immortal purpose, Thou redeemest thy children and leadest them on into life and growth and development and joy that cease not with this bit of experience, but go on into other and greater modes of experience of which we have now but instincts and intuitions and brave and aspiring confidences. Help me to live in that confidence, O my God, and to find in it daily inspiration. In the name of Jesus Christ. Amen.*

TO ESTABLISH MENTAL HABITS

I will trust in the covert of thy wings.   PSALM 61:4

Read PSALM 61

There is no new technique for entrance upon this stage where the soul in its deeper levels is continuously at Home in Him. The processes of inward prayer do not grow more complex, but more simple. In the early weeks we begin with simple, whispered words. Formulate them spontaneously, "Thine only. Thine only." Or seize upon a fragment of the Psalms: "So panteth my soul after Thee, O God." Repeat them inwardly, over and over again. But the time will come when verbalization is not so imperative, and yields place in the attitudes of soul which you meant the words to express, attitudes of humble bowing before Him, attitudes of lifting high your whole being before Him that the light may shine into the last crevice and drive away all darkness, attitudes of approach and nestling in the covert of his wings, attitudes of amazement and marvel at his transcendent glory, attitudes of feeding in an inward Holy Supper upon the Bread of Life.

PRAYER: *O my God, the strength of all who put their trust in Thee, I want to live in a way that is continuously at Home in Thee, and pray that Thou wilt give me an ever-renewed vision of life as Thou wouldst have me live it. In the name of Jesus Christ. Amen.*

59TH DAY

SHUT OUT ALL BUT GOD

Thou, when thou prayest, enter into thy closet, and when thou hast shut thy door, pray to thy Father which is in secret.   MATTHEW 6:6

Read MATTHEW 6:5-8

You need not go to heaven to see God, or to regale yourself with God. Nor need you speak loud as if He were far away. Nor need you cry for wings like a dove so as to fly to Him. Settle yourself in solitude, and you will come upon God in yourself. . . . Those who can in this manner shut themselves up in the little heaven of their own hearts . . . they lay their pipe right up to the fountain.

PRAYER: *O Lord, my God, Light of the minds that see Thee, Life of the souls that love Thee, and Strength of the thoughts that seek Thee; enlarge my mind, I pray, and raise the vision of my heart, and give me swift wings of thought, so that my spirit may reach Thee, the Eternal Wisdom, who art from everlasting to everlasting. Open my heart to every call from Thee, and when worldly fears come upon me let thy light lead me into right ways. In the name of Jesus Christ. Amen.*

LIGHT CAN BE HAD

O send out thy light and thy truth: let them lead me.   PSALM 43:3

Read PSALM 43

I am convinced, as I look back, that there were many occasions in that dynamic period when I was the recipient of Light and Leading above and beyond any wisdom of my own. I had no ecstatic experiences, I was subject to no miraculous-seeming revelations. No sharp break occurred in the unfolding steps of a normal and ordinary life. I could not have said: "Here and here an angel of God met me in the road or wrestled with me in the dark." I have few epoch-dates to record and no single Damascus vision. What I do feel sure of, however, is a frequent influx of divine life and power—the warm and intimate touch of a guiding Hand. I somehow felt all through these college years that I was being *prepared for something.* There was a dim but growing consciousness of mission.

PRAYER: *Infinite Father, help me to see my calling. To the great battle-field between right and wrong, help me to bring, in my day, through a character begotten of God, something of the benignity, the beauty, the saving grace of the Eternal Spirit; make me a portion of the moral might by which the world is brought from darkness to light. And to Thee be the glory. Amen.*

RIGHT THINKING
ABOUT YOURSELF

What is man, that thou art mindful of him? . . .
Thou hast made him a little lower than the angels.
PSALM 8:4, 5

Read PSALM 8

Christianity teaches that we are personal centres
of the One Universal Life, and that as such we live
to help God, to be the means of his self-realization
and self-expression, to be the instrument of the
Divine Will for the complete and permanent es-
tablishment of a Kingdom of love upon the earth.
. . . We are in the world as conscious, individuated
centres of His own Creative Life, and as such, God
needs us as we need Him. He has poured his own
being into us that in and through us He might come
to his own fullest realization and expression.

PRAYER: *Holy, holy, holy, Lord God Almighty,
Source of my life and Supply of every need, I worship Thee, I adore Thee. O thou enfolding Life
and Mind and Spirit and mysterious Presence, I
commit myself to Thee. O mighty Power of God,
make Thyself manifest in my life today. And to
Thee, my God, be praise and worship forever and
ever. Amen.*

I AM SOUGHT BY GOD

I . . . heard a voice saying unto me, Saul, Saul?
ACTS 22:7

Read ACTS 26:1-20

Less and less, I think, grows the consciousness of
seeking God. Greater and greater grows the certainty that He is seeking us and giving Himself to
us to the completest measure of our present capacity.
. . . There is such a thing as putting ourselves in
the way of God's overflowing love and letting it
break upon us till the response of love comes, not
by struggle, not even by deliberation, but by necessity, as the echo comes when the sound strikes the
rock.

PRAYER: *O Thou who, in the greatness of thy
love, art forever seeking to draw to Thyself the
souls of men, forgive me that I have so often failed
to listen to thy voice when thou hast called, and help
me from this time forward to be quickly responsive
to thy every approach. O my God, I open to Thee
the ears of my understanding, I throw wide open
to Thee the door of my soul. Make me to be thoroughly thine. In the name of Jesus Christ. Amen.*

I MUST BECOME ORGANIZED

And the Lord opened the eyes of the young man.
II KINGS 6:17

Read II KINGS 6:8-17

I was on a solitary walk, absorbed with my
thoughts about the meaning and purpose of my life,
wondering whether I should ever get myself organized and brought under the control and direc-
tion of some constructive central purpose of life,
when I felt the walls between the visible and the
invisible suddenly grow thin, and I was conscious
of a definite mission of life opening out before me.
I saw stretch before me an unfolding of labor in
the realm of mystical religion, almost as clearly as
Francis heard himself called at St. Damiens to "re-
pair the Church." I remember kneeling down alone
in a beautiful forest glade and dedicating myself
then and there in the quiet and silence, but in the
presence of an invading Life, to the work of interpreting the deeper nature of the soul and its relation with God.

PRAYER: *O Thou who art the Guide into true
life, help me so to forget the things which are behind and to stretch forward to the things which are
before, that I shall worthily run the race that is set
before me and do in the world that portion of thy
work which I am able to do as I press on toward the
goal unto the prize of the high calling of God in
Christ Jesus. Amen.*

OPEN THE SLUICES

For him, and through him, and to him, are all things.   ROMANS 11:36

Read ROMANS 11:33-36

"The reason why men find it hard to regard prayer in the same light in which it was formerly regarded is, that *we* seem to know more of the unchangeableness of Law: but I believe that God reveals Himself in each individual soul. Prayer is, to take a mundane simile, like opening a sluice between the great ocean and our little channels when the great sea gathers itself together and flows in at full tide." . . . He [Tennyson] said that "O Thou Infinite, Amen" was the form of prayer which he himself used in the time of trouble and sorrow.

PRAYER: *O Thou everlasting Source of Life, Thou hast set in my heart a restlessness that forbids me to be satisfied with what I have made of life. Help me, then, to open the channels between the great ocean of Thyself and the great need in myself, and let thy wisdom and inspiration and strength flow into me in full tide. Take hold upon me and within me with thy might mightily at all times, whether of darkness or of light, so that thy will shall be accomplished in me, and for me, and through me, for my own good and for the good of the world. In the name of Jesus Christ. Amen.*

LET GOD'S POWER WORK

According to the power that worketh in us.   EPHE-
SIANS 3:20

Read EPHESIANS 3:14-21

I lean closer and closer as life goes on. I feel that
our hope lies in despair—despair of self. The ves-
sels which contain the treasure are earthen, "that
the excess of the power may be God's and not from
us." And there *is* a power, there is a life working in
us. It is the quiet, sane, constant work of the Spirit
in and upon our spirit, that never hastes and never
tires: which gives me comfort. The same life that is
at work in the hedge across the road is in us, only in
us it attains full self-consciousness and freedom. We
can deliberately use it or refuse it.

PRAYER: *O Thou who art over all, and in all, and
through all, help me all through this day and continually to walk in awareness of Thee, and in mystic
communion with Thee, and in profound union with
Thee, and in quick and sure responsiveness to Thee.
And let thy power work in me and through me
without ceasing. Amen.*

STRAIGHT OUT TOWARD GOD

The Lord is my portion, saith my soul; therefore will I hope in him.   LAMENTATIONS 3:24

Read LAMENTATIONS 3:22-26

I cannot find the word that will mean to you or to me what I am now experiencing. It is a will act. I compel my mind to open straight out toward God. I wait and listen with determined sensitiveness. I fix my attention there, and sometimes it requires a long time early in the morning to attain that mental state. I determine not to get out of bed until that mind set, that concentration upon God, is settled. It also requires determination to keep it there. But for the most part recently I have not lost sight of this purpose for long and have soon come back to it. After a' while, perhaps, it will become a habit, and the sense of effort will grow less.

PRAYER: *Unto the King eternal, incorruptible, invisible, the only God, be honor and glory forever and ever. My trust is in Thee. Help me to keep my mind at all times open straight out toward Thee. And to Thee be glory forever. Amen.*

FOOD FOR DAILY LIVING

I am that bread of life.   JOHN 6:48

Read JOHN 6:41-51

Thee when I first knew, Thou liftedst me up, that I might see there was what I might see, and that I was not yet such as to see. And Thou didst beat back the weakness of my sight, streaming forth thy beams of light upon me most strongly, and I trembled with love and awe: and I perceived myself to be far off from Thee, in the region of unlikeness, as if I heard this thy voice from on High: "I am the food of grown men; grow, and thou shalt feed upon Me; nor shalt thou convert Me, like the food of thy flesh, into thee, but thou shalt be converted into Me."

PRAYER: *Infinite Father, I thank Thee that thou hast made Thyself essential to human life, and that I seek Thee because all the higher instincts of my humanity cry out unto Thee, thou living God; and I thank Thee that as I travel toward Thee I find that thou art coming toward me with the welcome of thy perfect love. Help me never to lose faith in the fundamental nature of man. Help me to a great faith and a great hope; and help me to render to Thee the harmonious, incessant worship of my heart. And to Thee be praise and honor and glory forever. Amen.*

THE PARAMOUNT OBLIGATION

A new commandment I give unto you, That ye love one another; even as I have loved you, that ye also love one another. By this shall all men know that ye are my disciples, if ye have love one to another. JOHN 13:34, 35

Read JOHN 13:31-35

One day when St. Catherine of Siena was sitting in the open air with her companions, a poor man came and asked for alms. When Catherine replied that she had no money to give him, he said she could give him her cloak. Without a moment's delay she took it off and put into his hands. In Siena a woman who appeared on the street without her mantle advertised herself as a public courtesan, and those who were sitting with Catherine would not permit her to subject herself to such disgrace and therefore redeemed the cloak, the beggar making them pay a high price for it. When Catherine was asked how she could have dared to think of appearing on the streets without her cloak, she responded: "I prefer to be without a cloak rather than without charity. . . . A person is of use to another creature to the extent that he loves him and no more, and he is wanting in service to the extent that he is wanting in love.

PRAYER: *O Lord, let that become possible to me by thy grace which by nature is impossible to me; through Jesus Christ. Amen.*

TO BECOME INVULNERABLE

I can do all things through Christ which strength-
eneth me.   PHILIPPIANS 4:13

Read PHILIPPIANS 4:10-13

Religious faith would be the best preventative
against the maladies of the soul and the most powerful means of curing them if it had sufficient life
to create true stoicism in its followers. In this state
of mind, which is, alas! so rare in the thinking
world, a man becomes invulnerable. Feeling himself upheld by God, he fears neither sickness nor
death. He may succumb under the attacks of physical disease, but morally he remains unshaken in the
midst of his sufferings, and is inaccessible to the
cowardly emotions of nervous people. I have experienced a deep sympathy for a poor Catholic missionary whom I advised not to return to the deadly
climate of Africa, and who replied to me, with
an angelic smile: "I will go back, doctor; it is my
duty, it is my life!"

PRAYER: *Eternal God, by whose Son it was said
that if we had sufficient faith we could remove
mountains, increase both my faith in the unchanging purpose of thy love, and my steadfastness in
the doing of thy will. In the name of Jesus Christ.
Amen.*

GOD'S WILL IS MY WILL

And Ruth said . . . whither thou goest, I will go; and where thou lodgest, I will lodge: thy people shall be my people, and thy God my God: Where thou diest, will I die, and there will I be buried: the Lord do so to me, and more also, if aught but death part thee and me.   RUTH 1:16, 17

Read RUTH 1:1-17

Dare to look up to God and say, "Make use of me for the future as Thou wilt. I am of the same mind. . . . I refuse nothing which seems good to Thee. Lead me whither Thou wilt. Clothe me in whatever dress Thou wilt. Is it thy will that I should be in a public or a private condition, dwell here or be banished, be poor or rich? Under all these circumstances I will make my defence to men. I will show what the nature of everything is."

PRAYER: *Infinite Father, I thank Thee for the joy of living and learning, and I pray that in following great teachers and in communion with great books I may come to the greatest. I pray also that Thou wilt make me to grow in knowledge, and in wisdom and insight. And I ask that Thou wilt help me to lift up my knowledge into service, into character, and into life, and to follow Him whose life is the Light of the world. In his name. Amen.*

AWARENESS OF GOD

I will love thee, O Lord my strength.   PSALM 18:1

Read PSALM 18:1-19

Among all the moods of the spirit, that of simple awareness is the most precious. The divine condition cannot be induced; but it can be wooed and waited on with a humble mind. Readiness and expectation can become habits of the heart. As I stand, with the lid of the garbage pail in one hand and my empty tin dish in the other, something arrests me. I look up wonderingly. Then—oh, beauty and sweetness of the summer day! serenity and detachment of the summer world! I am invaded, flooded by it, caught away into it, dazzled by its exceeding loveliness. Before me the orchard lies peaceful and green, with birds in its widely branching old trees, crickets and butterflies in its grass, blue sky above it and golden sunshine irradiating it. Beside me is the glowing garden, and beyond are the untroubled hills. . . . Could we, if we tried, be aware more frequently? Doubtless we could and should. The whole trend of evolution seems to lie away from blindness and nescience toward intelligence; away from the partial toward the whole.

PRAYER: *O my God, Thou art with me, I am with Thee. Help me to live this day in awareness of Thee, and mystic communion with Thee, and profound union with Thee, and in quick and sure*

*responsiveness to Thee. In the name of Jesus Christ.
Amen.*

HOLD THE VISION CLEAR

And the Spirit bade me go with them.   ACTS 11:12

Read ACTS 11:1-18

Sometimes one withdraws for a moment into one's self, stepping aside from all of one's own intense activity to look on in amazement at the great pageantry of life flowing past. The spirit of life is through it all, and life is God, and God is love—ecstasy! Not a sparrow falls to the ground without your Father in Heaven—of course not! How could it, since He is there at its very heart? Call not thou anything common or unclean—Oh, I will not! I will not! I will hold the vision clear. How stupid I am, how blind most of the time! But to-day my eyes are open; I am moving in the mystery of life. I must hold the vision, recapturing it every morning, every day plunging it more and more into each act of life. I see how all of life should be glorified by the realization of this life more abundant, pouring into every activity, recreating all with joy.

PRAYER: *O Thou who hast been the Inspirer of men in all generations, give me today the inspiration I have need of. Speak to me, and if Thou hast special instructions make them known unto me.*

*And help me to hold the vision clear all through
the day. In the name of Jesus Christ. Amen.*

HABITUAL ORIENTATION

Our fellowship is with the Father, and with his
Son Jesus Christ.   1 JOHN 1:3

Read 1 JOHN 1:1-4

Longer discipline in this inward prayer will establish more enduring upreachings of praise and
submission and relaxed listening in the depths,
unworded but habitual orientation of all one's self
about Him who is the Focus. The process is much
simpler now. Little glances, quiet breathings of
submission and invitation suffice. Voluntary or
stated times of prayer merely join into and enhance
the steady undercurrent of quiet worship that un-
derlies the hours. Behind the foreground of the
words continues the background of heavenly orientation, as all the currents of our being set toward
Him. Through the shimmering light of divine
Presence we look out upon the world, and in its
turmoil and its fitfulness, we may be given to respond, in some increased measure, in ways dimly
suggestive of the Son of Man.

PRAYER: *Almight God, who art the Light of
the minds that know Thee, the joy of the hearts that
love Thee, and the Strength of the lives that serve*

Thee; help me so to know Thee that I may truly love Thee, so to love Thee that I may joyfully serve Thee; through Jesus Christ my Lord. Amen.

74TH DAY

LIFE ABUNDANT

I am come that they may have life, and that they might have it abundantly.   JOHN 10:10

Read JOHN 10:7-10

To love God might commence to be expressed as being a great quiet, an intense activity, a prodigious joy, and the poignant knowledge of *the immensity of an amazing new life shared.* Because of this new way of living, the mind acquires a great increase of capacity and strength and clearness: being able to deal quickly and correctly with all matters brought before it with an ease previously altogether unknown to its owner. It is no exaggeration to say that the sagacity, scope, and grasp of the mind feels to be more than doubled from that which it previously was, and this not because of any study, but by an involuntary alteration. Those who feel desire and need within themselves to reach the heights of inward life will do it best, not through diversity of interests in fellow-creatures, but by unification of all interests in God.

PRAYER: *O Lord God, who hast called me to ventures of which I cannot see the ending, by paths as yet untrodden and through perils unknown: give me faith to go out with good courage, not knowing whither but only that thy hand is leading and thy love supporting me. Amen.*

THE HAUNTING PRESENCE

The God of glory thundereth. . . . The voice of the Lord is full of majesty. . . . And in his temple doth every one speak of his glory.   PSALM 29:3, 4, 9

Read PSALM 29

Move where he will, there is a thought and a Presence which [man] cannot put aside. He is haunted forever by the Eternal Mind. God looks out upon him from the clear sky and through the thick darkness, is present in the raindrop that trickles down the branches and in the tempest that crashes down the forest. A living Redeemer stands beside him, goes with him, talks with him as a man with his friend.

PRAYER: *O Thou before whom I bow myself in awe, Source of all being, Fount of all Life, Transcendent, Eternal, and yet as near as my own soul: help me to realize thy nearness as I go through this day, and let enlargement come to this spirit of mine by association with thy gracious and eternal Spirit. Cleanse my thoughts and uplift and greaten my outlook on life by the breathing in of thy Spirit abun-*

75

dantly, O my God; and take out of me all unclean-
ness, all meanness, all pettiness, all hardness, all
unkindness, all wish to hurt another, all cruelty of
any kind—and all else that is not good. O give me
deliverance, my God and Savior. Amen.

GOD-GIVEN IMPULSES

I have prayed for thee, that thy faith fail not.　LUKE
22:32

Read LUKE 22:54-62

I cast myself down I know not how, under a
certain fig tree, giving full vent to my tears; and I
sent up these sorrowful words: How long? how
long, "tomorrow, and tomorrow?" Why not now?
So was I speaking, and weeping in the most bitter
contrition of my heart, when, lo! I heard from a
neighboring house a voice, as of boy or girl, I know
not, chanting, and oft repeating, "Take up and read;
Take up and read." So checking the torrent of my
tears, I arose; and interpreting it to be no other
than a command from God, to open the book, and
read the first chapter I should find. Eagerly then I
returned to the place where Alypius was sitting;
for there had I laid the volume of the Apostle, when
I arose thence. I seized, opened, and in silence read
that section, on which my eyes first fell: *Not in*
rioting and drunkenness, not in chambering and

wantonness, not in strife and envying: but put ye on the Lord Jesus Christ, and make not provision for the flesh. Instantly at the end of this sentence, by a light as it were of serenity infused into my heart, all the darkness of doubt vanished away.

PRAYER: *O God, my Savior, help me to keep the ears of my spirit ever open to Thee, so that I may not at any time fail to perceive the calling of thy voice. In the name of Jesus Christ. Amen.*

77TH DAY

GOD ALWAYS, ALWAYS GOD

Thou God seest me. GENESIS 16:13

Read GENESIS 16:1-16

Pray remember what I have recommended to you, which is, to think often on God, by day, by night, in your business, and even in your diversions. He is always near you and with you: leave Him not alone. . . . Think on Him often, adore Him continually, live and die with Him; this is the glorious employment of a Christian. In a word, this is our profession; if we do not know it, we must learn it. . . . We cannot escape the dangers which abound in life without the actual and *continual* help of God: let us then pray to Him for it *continually.* How can we pray to Him without being with Him? How can we be with Him but in thinking of Him often? And how can we often think of Him, but by a holy habit which we should form of it? . . . We must *know* before we can *love*. In order to *know* God, we must often *think* of him.

PRAYER: *To think of Thee, O Lord, my God, is to rest; to know Thee is eternal life; to serve Thee is the realization of life's purpose and a deep joy. Therefore I come to Thee, and I ask that Thou wilt fill me with the apprehension of Thee that I need, and with abundance of thy mind and spirit. And to Thee be glory. Amen.*

78TH DAY

POSSESSING GOD IN TRANQUILLITY

And he said, My presence shall go with thee.
EXODUS 33:14

Read EXODUS 33:7-14

[Brother Lawrence said] That we should establish ourselves in a sense of God's Presence, by continually conversing with Him. . . . That he was more united to God in his outward employments, than when he left them for devotion in retirement. . . . "The time of business," said he, "does not with me differ from the time of prayer; and in the noise and clatter of my kitchen, while several persons are at the same time calling for different things, I possess God in as great tranquility as if I were upon my knees at the blessed sacrament."

PRAYER: *Bless me, O Lord Eternal, with the vision of thy being and beauty, so that in the joy and strength of that vision I may do my work as a service both to Thee and to my fellow men, without impatience or restlessness, but in love and joy. Quicken and deepen in me the consciousness of thy Presence, and refresh me with thy power. Help me to live continually in the realization that I am in thy service and keep me humble by revealing to me my littleness and my failings, but let me never forget that Thou art my Counselor, my Savior, and my Friend. In the name of Jesus Christ. Amen.*

79TH DAY

FUSION WITH GOD

And there appeared unto them cloven tongues like as of fire, and it sat upon each of them.   ACTS 2:3

Read ACTS 2:1-4

How can a Contact with God be in any way described? It is not seeing, but meeting and fusion with awareness. The soul retaining her own individuality and consciousness to an intense degree, but imbued with and fused into a life of incredible intensity, which passes through the soul vitalities and emotions of a life so new, so vivid, so amazing, that she knows not whether she has been embraced by love or by fire, by joy or by anguish. . . . The heat of Christ is mixed with indescribable sweetness:

giving marvellous pleasure and refreshment and happiness, and wonderfully adapted to the delicacy of the human creature. The heat of the Godhead is very different, and sometimes we may even feel it to be cruel and remorseless in its very terrible and swift intensity. But the soul, like all great lovers, never flinches or hangs back.

PRAYER: *O Lord, my God, let thy life engulf me, thy strength sustain me, thy light give me light continually, thy Holy Spirit direct me at all times, and thy peace enfold me. And to Thee be glory forevermore. Amen.*

80TH DAY

I WILL ABSORB THE LIGHT

They need no candle, neither light of the sun; for the Lord God giveth them light.   REVELATION 22:5

Read REVELATION 22:1-5

I saw my soul under the image of a very limpid stretch of water and above that water God appeared like an incomparable Star, whose light was more brilliant than that of the sun and gentler than that of the moon. Not only did the light irradiate all the surface of the water, but the water iself was so transparent that the rays of this light penetrated into its very depths. And these depths seemed to be inlaid with precious stones, which glittered through the water under the rays of the mysterious Star. With what ardour the light penetrated the water; with what love the water absorbed the light, I cannot find words to say! God made me understand that the fusion of these two elements was only an imperfect figure of the union which exists between Him and my soul, when through His Divine love she is made, as it were, one spirit with Him.

PRAYER: *O Thou who art the Source of all light, Thou who givest light to the heavens, and light to the mind, and light to the spirit: send forth into me the light of thy truth, and thy love, and save me from that worst of all darkness which is darkness of soul. In the name of Jesus Christ. Amen.*

81ST DAY

I MUST BECOME A NEW CREATURE

Therefore if any man be in Christ, he is a new creature.   II CORINTHIANS 5:17

Read II CORINTHIANS 5:14-19

Then said our good Lord Jesus Christ: "Art thou well paid that I suffered for thee?" I said: "Yea, good Lord, gramercy. Yea, good Lord, blessed mayst thou be." Then said Jesus, our kind Lord: "If thou art paid, I am paid: it is a joy, a bliss, an endless liking to me that ever suffered I passion for thee; and if I might suffer more, I would suffer more." . . . And in these words: "If that I might suffer more, I would suffer more," —I saw soothly that as often as he might die, so often he would, and love should never let him have rest till he had done it. And I beheld with great diligence for to learn how often he would die if he might. And soothly the number passed mine understanding and my wits so far that my reason might not, nor could comprehend it. And when he had thus oft died, or should, yet he would set it at naught for love: for all seemeth him but little in comparison with his love.

PRAYER: *I beseech thee, O Lord, that the fiery and sweet strength of thy love may absorb my soul from all things that are under heaven, that I may die for love of thy love as Thou didst deign to die for love of my love. Amen.*

82ND DAY

CHRIST'S MIND IN ME

Let this mind be in you, which was also in Christ Jesus. PHILIPPIANS 2:5

Read PHILIPPIANS 2:1-11

But apparently my Bridegroom, Eternal Truth, has wished to put me to a very sweet and genuine test, inward and outward, in the things which are seen and those which are not—the latter beyond count the greater. But while He was testing us, He cared for us so gently as tongue could not tell. Therefore I wish pains to be food to me, tears my drink, sweat my ointment. Let pains make me fat, let pains cure me, let pains give me light, let pains give me wisdom, let pains clothe my nakedness, let pains strip me of all self-love, spiritual and temporal. The pain of lacking consolations from my fellow-creatures has called me to consider my own lack of virtue, recognizing my imperfection, and the very perfect light of Sweet Truth, who gives and receives, not material things, but holy desires.

PRAYER: *Help me, my God and Savior, to lay aside all encumbrance, and to take with patience and strength all the tests that life shall bring, as the follower of Him who for the joy that was set before Him endured the Cross, and went on to the high consummation of life in thy Eternal Realm. In his Name I ask. Amen.*

83RD DAY

GOD THE CENTER OF ALL CREATION

Lift up your eyes on high, and behold who hath created these things.   ISAIAH 40:26

Read ISAIAH 40:26-31

And after this I saw God in a Point, that is to say, in mine understanding,—by which sight I saw that he is in all things. And all this he shewed me full blissfully, meaning thus: "See! I am God: see! I am in all thing: see! I do all thing: see! I lift never my hands off my works, nor ever shall, without end: see! I lead all thing to the end I ordained to it from without beginning, by the same Might, Wisdom and Love whereby I made it. How should any thing be amiss?"

He shewed him [self] divers times reigning . . . but principally in man's soul. He hath taken there his resting-place and his worshipful City: out of which worshipful See he shall never rise nor remove without end.

Marvellous and solemn is the place where the Lord dwelleth, and therefore he willeth that we readily answer to his gracious touching, more rejoicing in his whole love than sorrowing in our often failings. For it is the most worship to him of anything that we may do, that we live gladly and merrily, for his love, in our penance.

PRAYER: *Help me, my God, to keep in my mind and soul continually that Point of light everlasting and to shape my life thereby. And to Thee be glory. Amen.*

SEEDS LEAD TO SHEAVES

He that goeth forth and weepeth, bearing precious seed, shall doubtless come again with rejoicing, bringing his sheaves with him. PSALM 126:6

Read PSALM 126

Often for days and weeks the doors of the spirit have been tight against me. I have lost the way. I cannot find the sacred citadel. I open door after door, and all the chambers are empty and desolate. Then suddenly, gloriously, pursuing some pathway of meditation, or in reading, I come upon an unexpected turn of thought, the way is opened, and there—there once more is the hidden treasure! A golden flood of love and sunshine, pouring itself out for me to bathe my starved, lonely, and frightened self in once more. I seem to be walking in a stream of sunlight, and my footsteps move to the rhythm of blank verse. I am so sure of God, of love, and of the spirit, that the thought that I had ever lost the feeling is almost laughable.

PRAYER: *O Lord, my God, help me now to find in Thee what I cannot find out of Thee—rest and peace and joy, which abide with me only as I abide in Thee. Lift up my soul above the weary round of harassing thoughts to awareness of Thee and to the atmosphere of thy eternal Presence, that there I may draw strength from thy eternal life continually. In the name of Jesus Christ, I ask. Amen.*

SERVE GOD WHERE YOU ARE

Well done, thou good and faithful servant: thou hast been faithful over a few things, I will make thee ruler over many things: enter thou into the joy of thy lord.   MATTHEW 25:21

Read MATTHEW 25:14-30

[Brother Lawrence said] That the most excellent method he had found of going to God, was that of doing our common business purely for the love of God. So likewise, in his business in the kitchen (to which he had naturally a great aversion), having accustomed himself to do everything there for the love of God, and with prayer, upon all occasions, for His grace to do his work well, he had found everything easy, during fifteen years that he had been employed there. He was always pleasing himself in every condition, by doing little things for the love of God.

PRAYER: *O Thou who callest me to do the work of thy Kingdom in the station in which I am placed, make me humble, loving, thoughtful, and ready both for whatsoever may befall and also for all responsibilities that shall come upon me. Not that Thou wilt keep me from hard things do I pray, but that Thou wilt help me to be faithful under all conditions and at all times: faithful to the best, faithful to high adventure in the living of life, and above all faithful to Thee. In the name of Jesus Christ. Amen.*

WE FAINT NOT

For which cause we faint not; but though our outward man perish, yet the inward man is renewed day by day. II CORINTHIANS 4:16

Read II CORINTHIANS 4:16-18

[Brother Lawrence said] That when sometimes he had not thought of God for a good while, he did not disquiet himself for it; but after having acknowledged his wretchedness to God, he returned to Him with so much the greater trust in Him, as he had found himself wretched through forgetting Him. That he had so often experienced the ready succors of Divine Grace upon all occasions, that from the same experience, when he had business to do, he did not think of it beforehand; but when it was time to do it, he found in God, as in a clear mirror, all that was fit for him to do. When outward business diverted him a little from the thought of God, a fresh remembrance coming from God invested his soul, and so inflamed and transported him that it was difficult for him to contain himself.

PRAYER: *O Lord, our heavenly Father, who orderest life for our eternal good, silence my murmurings, quiet my fears, and dispel my doubts, so that, rising up out of all forgetfulness of Thee, I shall both consciously and subconsciously rest in Thee, thou Rock of everlasting strength. Through Jesus Christ. Amen.*

WE MUST CULTIVATE PURITY

Blessed are the pure in heart: for they shall see God. MATTHEW 5:8.

Read MATTHEW 5:1-12

God inflames the soul with a burning desire for absolute purity. One burns for complete innocency and holiness of personal life. No man can look on God and live, live in his own faults, live in the shadow of the least self-deceit, live in harm toward his least creatures, whether man or bird or beast or creeping thing. The blinding purity of God in Christ, how captivating, how alluring, how compelling it is! The pure in heart shall see God? More, they who see God shall cry out to become pure in heart, even as He is pure, with all the energy of their souls.

PRAYER: *Lord God, whose goodness is inexhaustible, Thou who art blessed forevermore, before whom stand ten thousand times ten thousand, and thousands of thousands, the hosts of angels and archangels and of the redeemed, search my heart and cast out of me every evil thought, every base desire, all envy and pride, all wrath and anger, every kind of impurity, and all that is contrary to thy Holy Will. And help me, O Lord, Lover of mankind, with a pure heart and contrite spirit to walk continually with Thee who art all-holy. Amen.*

GIVEN OVER TO GOD'S USE

Then said I, Lo, I come: I delight to do thy will, O my God. PSALM 40:7, 8

Read PSALM 40:1-10

I would fain to be to the Eternal Goodness, what his own hand is to a man.

PRAYER: *Holy, holy, holy, Lord God Almighty, who hast been, and who art, and who shalt be forevermore. I worship Thee, I adore Thee, I lift up my heart and my soul unto Thee, I humble myself before Thee. Enter into my mind, I pray, and help me to think thy thoughts. Enter into my heart, and fill it with the divine attitude toward all things. Enter into my body, and strengthen it with thy strength. Enter into my soul, and enlighten it with thy everlasting light. Help me to make myself a sanctuary of thy Spirit. And to Thee, and the Lord Jesus Christ, and the Holy Spirit, be honor and glory, world without end. Amen.*

NO STING FOR THOSE WHO TRUST

For this corruptible must put on incorruption, and this mortal must put on immortality. I CORINTHIANS 15:53

Read I CORINTHIANS 15:50-58

But it is the falling of the leaves that sets the seal upon the beautiful, significant process. In the beginning, a few at a time, they come drifting, circling downward, utterly careless and unobtrusive, yet deeply purposeful. With a sigh they seek the warm, pungent earth which is to them the ultimate breast of God. Death: it is just that. The word which we all avoid and disparage, yet which is surely one of the most beautiful words in our language. O dear, dim Goal, which incites in us such longing, what wilt thou do with us when we shall have found thee? Allow us to rest in thy freedom and know thy immensity, or send us forth again to work among the shows of things? That is no concern of ours, that is thy business, we must leave it to thee.

PRAYER: *O God of all grace, grant unto me thy peace which passeth understanding, so that the quietness which comes from friendship with Thee may possess my soul. Through Jesus Christ. Amen.*

WITH CHRIST TODAY

When the doors were shut where the disciples were assembled for fear of the Jews, came Jesus and stood in the midst, and saith unto them, Peace be unto you.   JOHN 20:19

Read JOHN 20:19-25

My friend at Stoke was ill: there was a bank holiday and I could visit him. He was not alone. Jesus was alive and present to my friend as he had been to the eleven in the upper room. He was alive and present to me. As this event has been the turning-point in my life, I have naturally examined it as thoroughly and tested it as ruthlessly as I can. What then can be said to make the facts more intelligible? I went to see my friend in an entirely normal state of mental and bodily health. He said nothing about religion: old times, old books, old comrades, of these we spoke, not of God. But it was evident that a third person was there: I do not know how else to express it. Jesus was objectively real, not subjectively realised. There was nothing strained or fantastic, abnormal or supernatural about it. Quite literally it was as simple and obvious as if my friend had had with him a revered and sympathetic colleague who listened to our talk and influenced our every movement by the atmosphere of his presence.

PRAYER: *Lord Christ, help me to walk in awareness of Thee continually though I see Thee not. Amen.*

GRATITUDE FOR SUFFERING

Now no chastening for the present seemeth to be joyous, but grievous: nevertheless afterward it yieldeth the peaceable fruit of righteousness unto them which are exercised thereby.   HEBREWS 12:11

Read HEBREWS 12:7-13

Next I find in these records a belief in the value of suffering, and gratitude that I have had it. The whole subject of suffering is too large a one to go into here, so I will merely say that perhaps not everyone needs it for development, but that undoubtedly I did, and, thank God!—no idle phrase —I *got* it. I would not *dare* to go through the world without some exercises in adversity which prod me awake, keep me from pulling the bedclothes of smug happiness up over my head and sinking into a comfortable and selfish repose. Like all natural human beings, I do not like to suffer, nor do I morbidly crave it for the good of my soul; but if I am heading for more of it, I hope that when it comes I shall meet it, not with resignation, which is a poor pale sister, but with enthusiasm.

PRAYER: *O Thou Holy One who inhabitest Eternity, Thou hast made me alive out of thine own life, and I give myself utterly to Thee. Help me to be so conscious of thy Everlasting Arms that I shall live my daily life at all times in the strength that comes from quietness and confidence. In the name of Jesus Christ. Amen.*

92ND DAY

HOW GREAT IS MY DESIRE?

The King of glory shall come in.   PSALM 24:7

Read PSALM 24:7-10

At Holy Communion my soul was immersed in such a complete and profound union that all her powers were suspended and lost in God. No definite attribute presented itself to my mind, only God in Himself, in his Thrice-Holy Unity, in his sublime Essence. . . . O Nature of God! It is impossible to say what Thou art. . . . All that can be said is that this august Majesty takes possession of the soul. . . . Our Lord has given me a most consoling instruction for souls who have not yet entered into the way of union. That is, "when He gives a soul an immense *desire* to possess Him, and when she corresponds with it, He finds Himself forced to accede to her desire and to grant her this intimate union." . . . I often noticed that an act of total and absolute abandonment to the Holy Will of God almost always draws down upon the soul the grace of union.

PRAYER: *O Thou who alone canst lift me up into true life, increase in me the desire for Thee, and lead me on from self-will to thy will, from the ephemeral to the eternal, from inconstancy to constancy, and from turbulence to the peace of Jesus Christ. Amen.*

93RD DAY

CONCENTRATED COMMUNION

I was in the Spirit.   REVELATION 1:10

Read REVELATION 1:10-18

The mode of entrance into active contemplation I would try to convey in this way. The body must be placed either sitting or kneeling, and supported, or flat on the back as though dead. Now the mind must commence to fold itself, closing forwards as an open rose might close her petals to a bud again, for every thought and image must be laid away and nothing left but a great forward-moving love intention. Out glides the mind all smooth and swift, and plunges deep, then takes an upward curve and up and on, and consciousness is taken over by the soul, which, quickly coming to the trysting-place, *spreads herself* and there awaits the revelations of her God. The creature worships, but the soul alone knows contact. And in this sublime adventure we are really conscious of no mode nor plan nor flight, nought but the mighty need of spirit to Spirit and love to Love.

PRAYER: *O Most Holy Trinity! help me to realize myself in thy Presence every hour, every minute, as much as it is possible to do so. Be the soul of my soul, the life of my life, the flame of my heart, the eye of my mind, the breath of my word, the strength of my patience, the nerve of my action. Amen.*

94TH DAY

GOD ALONE

The Lord, The Lord God, merciful and gracious, longsuffering, and abundant in goodness and truth.
EXODUS 34:6

Read EXODUS 34:1-8

I desired to see *God alone,* and He consented and gave *Himself alone,* manifesting Himself without any intermediary. After this unspeakable meeting with God, the soul . . . has *felt, seen,* in a certain manner that God is the *Principle of all things,* that He is *other than all things, alone* amidst all that exists, and alone *He Who Is.* The soul knows Him *by this* and by no other reasoning or comparison. Inasmuch as it is possible for her to see Him, she sees Him *through Himself,* and *without intermediary.* This partial vision of God which she dimly perceives is, however slight, indeed *God.* Thenceforth she knows God independently of all reasoning and of the light of faith; formerly she *reasoned,* she *believed,* now she *sees.* What she has dimly *perceived* concerning the *Divine Nature,* reveals God to her as infinitely above all, and *distinct* from all that exists, and *altogether other.*

PRAYER: *O Thou who doest great things past finding out, yea, marvelous things without number, open the eyes of my soul, I pray, and give me understanding of the way in which I can think of Thee aright. In the name of Christ Jesus. Amen.*

95TH DAY

PRACTICE THE THOUGHT OF GOD

When he hath tried me, I shall come forth as gold. My foot hath held his steps. JOB 23:10, 11

Read JOB 23:3-11

The habit of living in union with God is not something that is possible only to a spiritually gifted few. It is a matter of practice. Ask a violinist how he gets his marvelous command over his fingers, and he says: "I practice, and practice, and practice!" Ask a spiritual man how he maintains his conscious union with God, and he tells you: "I practice the thought of God." What he means is that as he engages in his task of chopping wood, or selling merchandise, or being a bank clerk, or writing a book, or doing housework and attending to the repeated insistencies of little children, he carries with him the thought of God's environing nearness. As he practices the habit he feels that he is not struggling all by himself. He finds himself the recipient, day by day and moment by moment, of energy that he tremendously needs: physical and mental and moral and spiritual energy that comes from the Everlasting Source of all life.

PRAYER: *My God! my God! I would have my thought of Thee greater, truer, more constant, more clear, more enlightened all the while. And to Thee be glory forever. Amen.*

96TH DAY

GOODNESS MUST BE COMPLETE

Hath the Lord as great delight in burnt offerings and sacrifices, as in obeying the voice of the Lord?
1 SAMUEL 15:22

Read 1 SAMUEL 15:1-22

God is the Being of all that are, and the Life of all that live, and the Wisdom of all the wise; for all things have their being more truly in God than in themselves, and also all their powers, knowledge, life, and all the rest; for if it were not so, God would not be all good. Now what is good is agreeable to

God, and He will have it. Therefore it cannot be contrary to Him. But what then is there which is contrary to God and hateful to Him? Nothing but Sin. But what is Sin? Mark this: Sin is nothing else than that the creature willeth otherwise than God willeth, and contrary to Him. When a man willeth otherwise than God, or contrary to God, whatever he doeth or leaveth undone, in short all that proceedeth from him, is contrary to God and is sin. As Christ said: "He that is not with Me is against me."

PRAYER: *O Thou God of all grace, make me perfect in every work to do thy will, and this day and every day work in me that which is well pleasing in thy sight. Through Jesus Christ, to whom be glory forever and ever. Amen.*

97TH DAY

WHEN THE MIND WANDERS

Casting all your care upon him; for he careth for you.   I PETER 5:7

Read I PETER 5:6-11

When the mind has contracted certain bad habits of wandering and dissipation [in prayer], they are difficult to overcome. I believe one remedy for this is to confess our faults, and to humble ourselves before God. I do not advise you to use multiplicity of words in prayer: many words and long discourses being often the occasions of wandering. Hold your-self in prayer before God, like a dumb or paralytic beggar at a rich man's gate. Let is be *your* business to keep your mind in the presence of the Lord. If it sometimes wander and withdraw itself from Him, do not much disquiet yourself for that: trouble and disquiet serve rather to distract the mind than help to re-collect it: the will must bring it back in tranquillity.

PRAYER: *Almighty and everlasting God, who art always more ready to hear than we to pray, pour down upon me the abundance of thy mercy; for-giving me those things whereof my conscience is afraid, and giving me those good things which I am not worthy to ask, but through the merits and mediation of Jesus Christ, thy Son, our Lord. Amen.*

98TH DAY

A GOD READY TO PARDON

Thou art a God ready to pardon, gracious and merciful, slow to anger, and of great kindness.
NEHEMIAH 9:17

Read NEHEMIAH 9:7-17

When thou seest thyself in fault, thou shouldest always, without losing time or beginning to reason about thy fall, drive away vain fear and cowardice, and this without disquieting or disturbing thyself. But thou shouldest recognize thy fault with humility, and turn with loving confidence to the Lord, place thyself in his Presence, ask his pardon in thy heart, and this without noise of words. If thou wouldest attain to a high degree of Perfection and inward Peace, thou must use the Weapon of Confidence in the Divine Goodness, night and day, and always when thou fallest. This humble and loving Conversation and complete Confidence in the Divine Mercy, thou must exercise in all the faults, imperfections, and failings that thou shalt commit, either advertently or inadvertently.

PRAYER: *O Thou Hope of the World, through thy help I will never lose my hope in Thee. For time and eternity, my Creator and Redeemer, I put my hope in Thee. Amen.*

99TH DAY

I AM CALLED TO SERVE

I heard the voice of the Lord, saying, Whom shall I send, and who will go for us? Then said I, Here am I; send me.   ISAIAH 6:8

Read ISAIAH 6:1-8

It struck me as incomprehensible that I should be allowed to lead such a happy life, while I saw so many people around me wrestling with care and suffering. Then one brilliant summer morning at Günsbach there came to me, as I awoke, the thought that I must not accept this happiness as a matter of course, but must give something in return for it. It must be directly human service. One morning in the autumn of 1904 I found on my writing-table in the College one of the green-covered magazines in which the Paris Missionary Society reported every month on its activities. That evening, in the very act of putting it aside that I might go on with my work, I mechanically opened this magazine. As I did so, my eye caught the title of an article: "The Needs of the Congo Mission." The writer expressed the hope that his appeal would bring some of those "on whom the Master's eyes already rested" to a decision to offer themselves for this urgent work. My search was over.

PRAYER: *Help me, my God, to hear and understand and follow thy calls as they come to me day by day. In the name of Jesus Christ. Amen.*

100TH DAY

AS LIGHTS IN THE WORLD

Do all things . . . that ye may be . . . the sons of God . . . shine as lights in the world.   PHILIPPIANS 2:14, 15

Read PHILIPPIANS 2:12-18

God must take to Himself all that is in me, within and without, so that there may be nothing in me which striveth against God or hindereth his work. Now if God took to Himself all men that are in the world, or ever were, and were made man in them, and they were made divine in Him, and this work were not fulfilled in me, my fall and my wandering would never be amended except it were fulfilled in me also. And in this bringing back and healing, I can, or may, or shall do nothing of myself, but just simply yield to God, so that He alone may do all things in me and work, and I may suffer Him and all his work and his divine will.

PRAYER: *O Thou Infinite and Eternal, though clouds and darkness are round about Thee, yet righteousness and judgment are the foundation of thy throne. I put my trust in Thee. When my weakness and ignorance incline me at times to fear, I still rest my hope in thy goodness; and in spite of all the mystery of life I give myself to Thee for all things, and forever. To Thee be praise. Amen.*

101ST DAY

MAKE COMMON TASKS A MINISTRY

God hath shewed me that I should not call any man common or unclean.   ACTS 10:28

Read ACTS 10:23-33

I was coming home after a long tramp and passed a crowd of shawl-clad women gathered round a dingy shop. The proprietor, in his shirt-sleeves, was dispensing packets of fish and chips wrapped in newspaper. The place was lit with naphtha flares, and misty with steam from his cooking; and the smell of damp humanity and stale food was heavy in the air. And again of a sudden the glory; and God fulfilling his eternal task, giving to his children their daily bread. The mothers of the poor, yes, and the huckster behind the counter, were his ministers, celebrating together an ancient and sacred rite. Men might make such traffic sordid and profane: it was not so, but a liturgy, and its celebrants had a high and holy calling.

PRAYER: *O Thou Everlasting Father, help me this day to perceive and understand somewhat of the greatness of the Divine purpose, so that both in spirit and in act I may be at one with thy holy will, and may perform that will without distinction of persons, as opportunity comes my way. In the Name of Jesus Christ. Amen.*

LARGER PERCEPTIONS

I wait for the Lord, my soul doth wait, and in his word do I hope.   PSALM 130:5

Read PSALM 130:1-6

Whether God sends suffering or not, I do not know. I only know that out of mine has come a larger perception of life, and at times a sense almost of intimacy with Him which I never knew before, and for which my whole being flows out in gratitude. . . . I have been seeing lovely things all my life, but they never presented themselves so poignantly as they have done since I entered into adversity. Now beauty appears as something more than itself. It seems to me a gateway into God. The thrilling, moving, tremendous thing about it is not the especial aspect under which it appears, not the tree, the flower, the bird note at dusk, but the occasional sense of otherwhereness, of something more, a marvelous Something—complete ecstasy— that the beauty half reveals. How may one put down in cold words what that Something is? O utter Love! I cannot, but I know! It is this overpowering Something that moves one so exquisitely, tears the heart out, almost terrifies at times by its nearness.

PRAYER: *O my God, greaten, I pray Thee, my perceptions, so that I shall become every day and increasingly awake to the realization of thy nearness. And to Thee be praise. Amen.*

103RD DAY

LEARNING TO LOVE GOD

Inasmuch as ye have done it unto one of the least of these my brethren, ye have done it unto me.
MATTHEW 25:40

Read MATTHEW 25:31-46

How shall I know that in very truth I am learning to love God whom I cannot see? What indeed is it for me—*to love God*? For my help and joy I am assured that He is in all my brothers of the common life, poor in their need, bestowing with their good gifts; and therefore they are more than mere messengers sent out from Him. Do I discern these manners of his display, and seek them with the strength of my desire? In so far I learn to love God. Do I shut them from my sight? Then I call upon a nominal God in vain, with my "Lord, Lord!" All men may discern God in his messengers, therefore all men may learn to love Him. By one thing only I can hide Him from myself—by the darkening of his light in my self-will, the narrowing of my eyelids to shut out that which does not serve some dominant and excluding interest of my narrow self.

PRAYER: *Send out thy light and thy truth, my God and Savior, and lead me out of all my ignorance, all my darkening of thy light, and fill me with true concern for all my fellows in life. In the name of Jesus Christ. Amen.*

104TH DAY

TRANSCENDENT GLORY

Glory ye in his holy name . . . seek his face continually.   1 CHRONICLES 16:10, 11

Read 1 CHRONICLES 16:1-14

In the language of religion worship is the recognition of the supreme worthfulness, the transcendent glory, of God. In worship a man's whole personality, all his powers of feeling, thought, and will, are focussed on the eternal life of the world, from which springs all that has power to stir the mind and move the heart, all Beauty, Truth, and Love. Worship is contemplation and adoration.

PRAYER: *O Thou Holy One who inhabitest eternity, I lift my thoughts to Thee in adoration. Thou hast given me life out of thine own life, and put into me the holy fire of aspiration to be filled from thy abundance and led continually by thy Spirit. And while I seek Thee here in this place, all over the world men and women are lifting hands and voices and longing hearts to Thee. Help them, O Lord. Enlighten and guide and bless all who seek Thee in any way, and lead us all into the kind of life that is salvation. In the name of Jesus Christ. Amen.*

105TH DAY

THE UPHOLDING SPIRIT

Make me to hear joy and gladness.   PSALM 51:8

Read PSALM 51

The vivid, continuous sense that God, the Spirit upholding our poor little spirits, is the true originator and the true end [of the soul's development] in all it may have of spiritual beauty, truth, goodness, and vitality; and that He it is who, however dimly yet directly, touches our souls and awakens them to that noblest, incurable discontent with our own petty self and to that sense of and thirst for the Infinite and Abiding which articulates man's deepest requirement: this is the experience without which all life, and life's centre, religion, are flat and dreary.

PRAYER: *O Thou eternal Savior, all my trust is in Thee. Fill me, I pray, with thy Spirit, without whom nothing is strong, and nothing is holy; and make use of me as it shall be thy pleasure to do, for the growth of thy Kingdom and the glory of thy Name. Empty me of self-will, and fill me with the passion for wisdom. Correct my judgment, stir up in me a holy zeal, increase my faith, intensify in me the spirit of love. Reveal to me the work Thou wouldst have me do each day, and give me the power to do it as thy true follower in the service of God and of man. To Thee be praise. Amen.*

106TH DAY

THE ETERNAL BIRTH

And the angel answered and said unto her, The Holy Ghost shall come upon thee, and the power of the Highest shall overshadow thee: therefore also that holy thing which shall be born of thee shall be called the Son of God.   LUKE 1:35

Read LUKE 1:26-38

I have been asked what God is doing in heaven? I answer, He has been giving his Son birth eternally, is giving him birth now and will go on giving him birth for ever, the Father being in childbed in every virtuous soul. . . . Every virtue of the just, every act done by the just, is nothing but the Son being begotten by the Father. The Father never stops, he is always trying to beget his Son in me. . . . God's being born within the soul is nothing but God's self-revelation to the soul in some new knowledge and in some new mode.

PRAYER: *Thou who gavest me a living soul, grant me that I receive not my soul in vain. Grant me that I receive not thy grace in vain, nor hope of thy holy things. Our fathers trusted in Thee: they trusted, and Thou didst deliver them. They cried unto Thee, and were delivered. As Thou didst our fathers in the generations of old, so also deliver me, O Lord, who trust in Thee. Amen.*

107TH DAY

THE COMING OF CERTITUDE

When I said, My foot slippeth; thy mercy, O Lord, held me up. PSALM 94:18

Read PSALM 94:1-19

I was ill nearly all this year, and at one time I was unable to go out of doors for six months. Many things combined to make me feel sad, and I complained to our Lord that He had abandoned me. One day as I was sitting alone doing some needle-

work, my mind full of these thoughts, my soul was
suddenly taken possession of and, as it were, flooded
by the Divine Presence. God was there, close to
me. I could not see Him, but I felt the certitude of
his Presence as a blind man is certain of the presence of some one whom he can hear and touch.

PRAYER: *O thou Infinite and Eternal, help me,
I pray, to the certitude of Thee that I need; and
pour into me now, and all through this day and
continually, thy life all through me, thy healing
power, thy sustaining power, thy energy, thy mind,
thy spirit, thy nature of outreaching, all-enfolding
love. And to Thee be glory forever. Amen.*

108TH DAY

THE ACCEPTANCE OF PAIN

Thy will be done in earth, as it is in heaven.
MATTHEW 6:10

Read MATTHEW 6:9-18

I saw something of the mystery of pain. I don't
suppose we can understand its meaning; but my
consolation was that it is not necessarily a sign of
God's displeasure—that the highest life was a life
of suffering, that the Son of Man was a "Man of
Sorrows." Everything seems to me to depend upon
the way in which one takes the pain—if one vol-
untarily says, "Thy kingdom come, Thy will be
done," then one is entering into the highest life, and

the pain becomes a new method of serving and knowing God. At any rate I hope a little first-hand experience of pain will make me more sympathetic. Pain seems to me now a greater mystery than ever before. But I comforted myself with the thought that in the highest Life ever seen on earth, there was a full measure of spiritual, mental, and physical pain. Also it was a comfort to feel that when one accepted, not simply with resignation but with faith, certain suffering, one was in sympathy with the will of the universe, "working together with God in some mysterious way."

PRAYER: *O God, my Savior, where I cannot understand help me at any rate to live victoriously, following the example of thy Son Jesus Christ. Amen.*

109TH DAY

GOD IS WITH ME, I AM WITH GOD

Be strong and of a good courage; be not afraid, neither be thou dismayed: for the Lord thy God is with thee whithersoever thou goest.   JOSHUA 1:9

Read JOSHUA 1:1-9

I am as certain as I live that nothing is so close to me as God. God is nearer to me than I am to my own self; my life depends upon God's being near me, present in me. . . . Father and Son expire their holy Breath, and once this sacred Breath inspires a man it remains in him, for he is essential and pneumatic. . . . Not God himself, not angels, nor any sort of creature is able to disjoin the soul who is in the image of God. That is true union, and therein lies true happiness. The statement that our Lord from time to time holds converse with good people and that they hear words or become impressed with the sense of certain sayings . . . should be accepted with reserve and judged upon their merits, for locutions of this kind are often due to a trick the soul has, when indulging in comfortable intuitions of divinity, of answering herself by a sort of reflex action.

PRAYER: *Infinite Father, I thank Thee that the meaning of my life is in thy purpose concerning me, and the realization of thy purpose more and more my happiness. Amen.*

PRAISING GOD WHEN ALL IS DARK

The jailor . . . thrust them into the inner prison, and made their feet fast in the stocks. And at midnight Paul and Silas prayed, and sang praises unto God. ACTS 16:23-25

Read ACTS 16:11-31

Epictetus, a freed slave living in Rome, was lame, probably as the result of some torture inflicted by his former master, and so poor that all he possessed was an earthen lamp, a pipkin, and a bed. See, then, what he says in one of his great *Discourses*: "If we had any understanding, ought we not, both in public and in private, to sing hymns, and speak well of the Deity, and rehearse his benefits? . . . This is my business. I do it. Nor will I ever desert this post as long as it is vouchsafed me; and I exhort you to join in the same song."

PRAYER: *Infinite Father, as I seek day by day to find my way through this world where the real and the seeming good are in tragic confusion into the light that is eternal, into truth, beauty, and goodness, O Thou in whom all truth, all beauty, and all goodness forever abide, give me this day and every day the light and guidance of the Spirit of Truth, and help me continually, as the days pass, to live more consciously, reverently, joyously, in Thee. Amen.*

I I ITH DAY

MORE OF CHRIST

Acknowledgment of the mystery of God, and of the Father, and of Christ; In whom are hid all the treasures of wisdom and knowledge. COLOSSIANS 2:2, 3

Read COLOSSIANS 2:1-7

My experience is closing into this, that I turn from everything to Christ. I think I get glimpses into his mind, and I am sure that I love Him more and more. A sublime feeling of a Presence comes upon me at times which makes inward solitariness a trifle to talk about.

PRAYER: *O Thou Christ of God, Thou wast slain, and hast redeemed us to God by thy blood out of every kindred, and tongue, and people, and nation. Worthy is the Lamb that was slain to receive power, and riches, and wisdom, and strength, and honour, and glory, and blessing. Blessing, and honour, and glory, and power, be unto Him that sitteth upon the throne, and unto the Lamb, for ever and ever. Amen.*

112TH DAY

GOD SPEAKS THROUGH REASON

Teach me, O Lord, the way of thy statutes; and I shall keep it unto the end.   PSALM 119:33

Read PSALM 119:1-8

There is a thought which I have often had in my mind; but I would now lay upon my mind a charge to have it oftener there: that the light of reason is the law of God; the voice of reason is the voice of God; we never have to do with reason, but at the same time we have to do with God; our submission to the rules of reason is an obedience to God. Let me as often as I have evident reason set before me, think upon it; the great God now speaks to me.

PRAYER: *Infinite Father, lead me to the fountain of light. Thou art light and in Thee is no darkness at all. Let the light that made the Lord Jesus the Light of the world flow into my life and bring forth a great, exalted, rich, tender, full-hearted experience, issuing in wisdom, in sympathy, and in loving influence upon my fellow men. Make my life a life of Christly incentive, by thy grace and by thy Spirit, upon the lives and hearts and happiness of my fellows in life, and help me in my life to sing forth the song of the mercies that are new every morning and fresh every evening. In the name of the great Redeemer. Amen.*

113TH DAY

WITH GOD IN THE NIGHT

God my maker, who giveth songs in the night.   JOB 35:10

Read JOB 35:1-10

Sometimes when one wakes in the night He is there. There is nothing extraordinary about it, nothing unnatural or emotional, only a feeling of complete happiness. One may tell Him everything, offering one's whole life in gratitude, and trying with affectionate thought to bring one's friends into the companionship. Doing so, one drifts off to sleep, and, awakening again much later, finds that the Presence is still there. At the time there is nothing

114

strange about it; it is only when the nearness is withdrawn that it seems astonishing that it could ever have been. Often this happens just as one awakes in the morning also, only then it is more fleeting. Probably it comes more easily at such times because then one is relaxed, and the mental and physical faculties are in abeyance; the spirit is not caught so fast in the flesh, and is therefore more alert.

PRAYER: *O Gracious and Holy Father, give me wisdom to perceive Thee, intellect to understand Thee, diligence to seek Thee, patience to wait for Thee, eyes to behold Thee, a heart to meditate upon Thee, and a life to proclaim Thee. Amen.*

114TH DAY

PRAYER ONETH THE SOUL TO GOD

My soul thirsteth after thee, as a thirsty land.
PSALM 143:6

Read PSALM 143:6-10

Prayer oneth the soul to God. For though the soul be ever like to God in kind and substance, restored by grace, it is often unlike in condition, by sin on man's part. Then is prayer a witness that the soul willeth as God willeth; and it comforteth the conscience and enableth man to grace. . . . When the soul is tempested, troubled, and left to itself by unrest, then it is time to pray, for to make itself supple and buxom to God. And this I saw: that what time we see needs wherefor we pray, then our good Lord followeth us, helping our desire; and when we of his special grace plainly behold him, seeing none other needs, then we follow him and he draweth us into him by love. And then shall we see God face to face, homely and fulsomely. The creature, that is made, shall see and endlessly behold God, which is the Maker.

PRAYER: *Teach me, Heavenly Father, that if I sincerely seek Thee I shall surely find Thee; and guide me in the way of confidence and trust. In the name of Jesus Christ. Amen.*

115TH DAY

GOD ALWAYS DRAWING

You . . . hath he [God] quickened together with him [Christ].   COLOSSIANS 2:13

Read COLOSSIANS 2:8-13

Then I turned my gaze upon myself, on what went on within me, and I remembered that I only lived at those times when I believed in God. As it was before, so it was now. I need only to be aware of God to live; I need only forget Him or disbelieve in Him, and I die. . . . "What more do you seek?" exclaimed a voice within me. "*This is He*. He is that without which one cannot live. To know God and to live is one and the same thing!"

PRAYER: *Vouchsafe to me, O Lord, the token of thy Presence, and give me continually the inspiration of thy Spirit of truth; for I am powerless when I depend upon my own self alone. Give to me the inward life, the power of discerning Thee at all times, the uprising of thy light within me, that I continually need; and help me to live with Thee all the while in hope, in faith, in love, and in great comfort. In the name of Jesus Christ. Amen.*

116TH DAY

"FEAR NOT"

There stood by me this night the angel of God, whose I am, and whom I serve, Saying, Fear not. ACTS 27:23

Read ACTS 27:18-26

When Sir Ernest Shackleton and his companions were shipwrecked on Elephant Island in 1914, he and two of the men set out to find help in order to keep the entire party from perishing. They had to cross eight hundred miles of Antarctic Ocean in an open whaleboat, and then to make a thirty-six-hour march over unknown mountains and glaciers on the island of South Georgia. Sir Ernest said afterward that although they were, during all that time, "comrades of death," they always felt that there was "Something Above"; and then he referred to the glorious 139th Psalm, and repeated the words which say: *If I take the wings of the morning, and dwell in the uttermost parts of the sea; even there shall thy hand lead me, and thy right hand shall hold me.* It often seemed to him, he declared, that the little company consisted not of three, but of four. And though he said nothing of his feeling to his companions, one of them told him afterward that as they made the march he had had the feeling that there was another Person with him.

PRAYER: *Bless the Lord, O my soul: and all that is within me, bless his holy Name. Holy, holy, holy, Lord God Almighty; heaven and earth are full of thy glory. Glory be to Thee, O Lord most high. Amen.*

117TH DAY

THE FUNDAMENTAL POWERS

But God hath chosen the foolish things of the world to confound the wise; and God hath chosen the weak things of the world to confound the things which are mighty; And base things of the world, and things which are despised, hath God chosen.
I CORINTHIANS 1:27, 28

Read I CORINTHIANS 1:18-29

As for me, my bed is made: I am against bigness and greatness in all their forms, and with the invisible molecular moral forces that work from individual to individual, stealing in through the crannies of the world like so many soft rootlets, or like the capillary oozing of water, and yet rending the hardest monuments of man's pride, if you give them time. The bigger the unit you deal with, the hollower, the more brutal, the more mendacious is the life displayed. So I am against all big organizations as such . . . against all big successes and big results; and in favor of the eternal forces of truth which always work in the individual and immediately unsuccessful way, under-dogs always, till history comes, after they are long dead, and puts them on the top.

PRAYER: *O Thou who art the First and the Last, make my littleness and weakness to serve thy purposes for the world, I pray. And to Thee be the glory. Amen.*

118TH DAY

WHAT GOD LOOKS FOR

Be ye therefore perfect, even as your Father which is in heaven is perfect. MATTHEW 5:48

Read MATTHEW 5:43-48

Not what thou art, nor what thou hast been, beholdeth God with his merciful eyes; but what thou wouldest be.

What do you think is his will? That we may become quite perfect and so be made one with Him and with his Father as He prayed we might be.

My wish is that I may perceive the God whom I

find everywhere in the external world, in like manner within and inside me.

PRAYER: *O Thou Infinite and Eternal, I thank Thee for the breath of life that Thou hast breathed into me. Help me, in whatever I am led to this day and all days, to meet it as thy true servant. Let me not shun it. Let me not shirk it. Let me not be a coward in the face of it. But let the Light of God enlighten me, the Wisdom of God direct me in my acts, the sense of God's glory fill my soul, the desire to do God's Will lift up my whole life. And to Thee be glory. Amen.*

119TH DAY

TAKE GOD IN THE GREAT WAY

The Lord God is my strength, And he will make my feet like hinds' feet, And he will make me to walk upon mine high places.   HABAKKUK 3:19

Read HABAKKUK 3:17-19

If the power to live valiantly is contingent upon worldly security and good health it is no power at all. Take God into your consciousness in the great way. Invite unceasingly into yourself what St. Paul speaks of as "all the fullness of God." Realize that you are surrounded by the sustaining life, the invigorating energy, the directive mind, the enfolding presence, the empowering Spirit, of the Infinite and Eternal. Make it your habit to think of God as desiring a genuine fulfillment of life for you. Think of him as desiring to have expression of himself through you. Do these things and you add to your struggling selfhood a great *plus* of power. Then you can lift yourself above the catastrophes of life and say with the ancient prophet: "Although the fig tree shall not blossom, neither shall fruit be in the vines; the labour of the olive shall fail, and the field shall yield no meat; the flock shall be cut off from the fold, and there shall be no herd in the stalls: Yet will I rejoice in the Lord, I will joy in the God of my salvation."

PRAYER: *O my God, renew my spirit and fill me with thy life, so that each day shall fill me with strength and joy. In the name of Jesus Christ. Amen.*

120TH DAY

TO KEEP YOURSELF UNSHAKABLE

Earnestly contend for the faith which was once delivered unto the saints.   JUDE 3

Read JUDE 17-25

Do you really want to live your lives, every moment of your lives, in his Presence? Do you long for Him, crave Him? Does every drop of blood in your body love Him? Does every breath you draw breathe a prayer, a praise to Him? Do you sing and dance within yourselves, as you glory to his love? Have you set yourselves to be his, and *only* his,

121

walking every moment in holy obedience? The fires of the love of God, of our love toward God, and of his love toward us, are very hot. Is love steadfastly directed toward God, in our minds, all day long? Do we intersperse our work with gentle prayers and praises to Him? Do we live in the steady peace of God, a peace down at the very depths of our souls, where all strain is gone and God is already victor over the world, already victor over our weaknesses? This life, this abiding, enduring peace that never fails, this serene power and unhurried conquest, inward conquest over ourselves, outward conquest over the world, is meant to be ours.

PRAYER: *O God, my Savior, help me to be so rooted and grounded in Thee that I may be strong for all the vicissitudes of life. I ask in the name of Jesus Christ. Amen.*

121ST DAY

THE WILL AND GOD

In all thy ways acknowledge him, and he shall direct thy paths.   PROVERBS 3:6

Read PROVERBS 3:1-7

I am taking by direct act of will, enough time from each hour to give God much thought. I am feeling God in each movement, by an act of will— willing that He shall direct these fingers that now strike this typewriter—willing that He shall pour through my steps as I walk—willing that He shall direct my words as I speak, and my very jaws as I eat! ... This sense of cooperation with God in little things is what so astonishes me, for I never have felt it this way before. I need something, and turn round to find it waiting for me. I must work, to be sure, but there is God working along with me. To know this gives a sense of security and assurance for the future which is also new to my life. My part is to *live this hour in continuous inner conversation with God and in perfect responsiveness to his will.*

PRAYER: *Speak to me, Lord, and I will listen and respond. When I have a decision to make or a judgment to pass, give me, I pray, the light that will keep me in harmony with Thee. Let me not walk in darkness, nor in half-light. Be Thou my light and my salvation in all things great and small. I ask in the name of Jesus Christ. Amen.*

122ND DAY

PRAYER FOR ALL MEN

Also we pray always for you ... That the name of our Lord Jesus Christ may be glorified in you, and ye in him.   II THESSALONIANS 1:11, 12

Read II THESSALONIANS 1:1-12

I cannot contentedly frame a prayer for my self in particular, without a catalogue for my friends; nor request a happiness, wherein my sociable disposition doth not desire the fellowship of my neighbour. I never hear the Toll of a passing Bell, though in my mirth, without my prayers and best wishes for the departing spirit; I cannot go to cure the body of my patient, but I forget my profession, and call unto God for his soul; I cannot see one say his prayers, but, in stead of imitating him, I fall into a supplication for him, who perhaps is no more to me than a common nature: and if God hath vouchsafed an ear to my supplications, there are surely many happy that never saw me, and enjoy the blessing of mine unknown devotions.

PRAYER: *O Hope of all the ends of the earth, and of them that are afar off upon the sea: O Thou in whom our fathers trusted, and Thou didst deliver them: remember thy whole creation for good. Live we or die we, Thou art our Lord; O Helper of the helpless, remember all who are in necessity and need thy succour. In the name of Jesus Christ. Amen.*

123RD DAY

GOD ALWAYS AT HAND

And the publican, standing afar off, would not lift up so much as his eyes unto heaven, but smote upon his breast, saying, God be merciful to me a sinner.
LUKE 18:13

Read LUKE 18:9-14

Anxiety and discouragement may easily come to people when they see how strict and diligent the

lives of our Lord Jesus Christ and his saints have
been, and that humanly we are not up to their level.
They think they are apart from God—so far apart
that they cannot follow him. Let no one think that!
No one may say at any time that he is apart from
God, either because of his faults, or infirmities, or
anything else. If, however, by reason of a great fault,
you are an outcast, so that you are not able to
approach God at all, then, of all times, consider that
God is near you, for great harm comes of feeling
that God is distant. For let a man go away or come
back, God never leaves.

PRAYER: *O God of hope, fill me, I beseech Thee,
with all joy and peace in believing, that I may ever
abound in hope by the power of thy Holy Spirit,
and show forth thankfulness to Thee in trustful and
courageous living. In the name of Jesus Christ.
Amen.*

124TH DAY

DEATH MEANS PROGRESS

This corruptible must put on incorruption, and this
mortal must put on immortality.   I CORINTHIANS
15:53

Read I CORINTHIANS 15:50-58

It is a brave act of valour to contemn death; but
where life is more terrible than death, it is then the
truest valour to dare to live. There is therefore but

one comfort left, that, though it be in the power of the weakest arm to take away life, it is not in the strongest to deprive us of death. The first day of our Jubilee is Death; we are happier with death than we should have been without it: for death is the cure of all diseases. There is no *Catholicon* or universal remedy I know, but this; which, though nauseous to queasie stomachs, yet to prepared appetites is Nectar, and a pleasant potion of immortality.

PRAYER: *Loving Father, support me all the day long of this troublous life until the shadows lengthen, and the evening comes, and the busy world is hushed, and the fever of life is over, and my work is done. Then in thy mercy grant me a safe lodging, and a holy rest in the place that thou hast prepared for those that love Thee. In the name of Jesus Christ. Amen.*

125TH DAY

THOU SHALT NOT BE OVERCOME

The Spirit also helpeth our infirmities.   ROMANS 8:26

Read ROMANS 8:26-30

Then shewed our good Lord words full meekly without voice and without opening of lips, right as He had afore done, and said full sweetly: "Thou shalt not be overcome." . . . And this word: "Thou shalt not be overcome," was said full clearly and full mightily, for assuredness and comfort against all tribulations that may come. He said not: "Thou shalt not be tempested, thou shalt not be travailed, thou shalt not be dis-eased"; but He said: "Thou shalt not be overcome." God willeth that we take heed to these words, and that we be ever mighty in sure trust, in weal and woe. For He loveth and liketh us, and so willeth He that we love and like Him and mightily trust in Him; and all shall be well.

PRAYER: *For the eternal love, ever seeking fuller entrance into my heart; for the grace which is sufficient for all my needs; for the joy no man can take from me; for the peace that passeth understanding; for the hope which is set before me; and for the promise of the Father's house, I thank Thee, O Lord my God; and especially for my Savior Jesus Christ. Amen.*

126TH DAY

TO BUILD THE SOUL

He that soweth to the Spirit shall of the Spirit reap life everlasting.   GALATIANS 6:8

Read GALATIANS 6:1-10

In a truly Godlike man his love is pure and unmixed, and full of kindness, insomuch that he cannot but love in sincerity all men and things, and wish well, and do good to them, and rejoice in their welfare. Yea, let them do what they will to such a man, do him wrong or kindness, bear him love or hatred or the like, yes, if one could kill such a man a hundred times over, and he always came to life again, he could not but love the very man who had so often slain him, and could not but wish well, and show him the very greatest kindness in his power, if the other would but only receive and take it at his hands. Neither may a man who is made a partaker of the divine nature, oppress or grieve anyone. That is, it never entereth his thoughts, or interests, or wishes, to cause pain or distress to any, either by deed or neglect, by speech or silence.

PRAYER: *O God of Love, give me to live interiorly with Thee above all things and to reflect Thee to others. Amen.*

127TH DAY

GUIDANCE

I will instruct thee and teach thee in the way which thou shalt go: I will guide thee with mine eye. PSALM 32:8

Read HEBREWS 11:1-10

In glancing back over this record I find that the first thing it brings me is a deep gratitude for guidance. Something—Some One—greater and wiser than I had a hand in it. Experiences came which I certainly did not invite, and indeed would have

avoided if I could have done so, but which nevertheless brought me such an awakening and widen-
ing of perception that I cannot but believe there
was a hidden intention in their coming. Incidents
came that held messages of truth, and also, as I
needed them, I found the right books and met the
right people. This assurance of guidance brings a
good heart for the future. If I was not deserted in
the past, neither shall I be in the days to come. The
whole scheme of life is greater than we know. There
are forces in touch with us that we do not suspect.

PRAYER: *Thanks and praise be unto Thee, my*
God and Savior, for the leadings that have come to
me again and again all through my life. Guide me
still, I pray, in things both great and small. I give
myself, mind and spirit and body, to Thee. And to
Thee be praise forevermore. Amen.

128TH DAY

REJOICE WHILE AT WORK

Rejoice in hope of the glory of God.   ROMANS 5:2

Read ROMANS 5:1-5

Everything came alike to him [Brother Lawrence]
every station, every duty. The good Brother found
God everywhere, as near when he was at the hum-
blest task as when praying with the Community. He
found no urgency for retreats, inasmuch as in
the common task he met the same God to love and

worship, as in the stillness of the desert. *His one method of going to* God *and abiding in his Presence was to do all for the love of Him*. It was a matter of no consequence to him, whether he was employed on one thing or the other, provided that therein he sought God's glory. It was to Him he looked, and not to the work in hand. He knew that the more opposed the task was to his inclination, the greater and more blessed was the love which made him sacrifice his will to God; that the *littleness* of the work lessened not one whit the value of the offering, for God *regards not the greatness of the work, but the love which prompts it*.

PRAYER: *O Thou who art Light Everlasting, give me light today for the making of every choice and the doing of every deed. Give me light as I think of the world and its needs. Give me light as I think of Thee. Help me to be a giver of light. And to Thee be the glory. Amen.*

129TH DAY

PRACTICE GOD'S PRESENCE

If I say, Surely the darkness shall cover me; even the night shall be light about me. Yea, the darkness hideth not from thee; but the night shineth as the day.   PSALM 139:11, 12

Read PSALM 139:1-12

Do you want to be delivered from fear of what life may bring? Practice the Presence of God.

Do you want your spirit to have a grip on peace under all circumstances and at all times? Practice the Presence of God.

Do you want daily wisdom for daily need? Practice the Presence of God.

Do you want your selfhood to become ripe and rich and beautiful, as it ought to? Practice the Presence of God.

Do you want to be an instrument for the building up of that better world for which we all long? Practice the Presence of God.

Keep yourself in mind and spirit in the Presence of God. Then go out into each day's life as an ambassador of the spirit of God, the mind of God, the love of God, the comfort of God.

PRAYER: *O my God, I thank Thee that I cannot flee from thy Presence or go from thy searching Spirit. Help me, I pray, to live continually in awareness of that Presence and that Spirit. Amen.*

130TH DAY

RECOLLECTION EVERYWHERE

Thou wilt shew me the path of life. PSALM 16:11

Read PSALM 16

You must take advantage of every odd moment; when you are waiting for someone, when you go from one place to another, when you are with people whose talk runs on, so that all you need to do is to let them talk, you can lift your heart to God for a moment and by so doing refresh yourself in the midst of your activities. The less time one has, the more important it is to manage it. If a person waits to have regular and convenient hours by himself, in order to fill them with serious things, he runs the risk of waiting too long. The life of prayer is not like the world's business. Worldly affairs need regular time freed for long consecutive application, but in one moment one can recall the presence of God, love Him, adore Him, offer Him what we are doing or what we are suffering, and in his presence calm all the agitations of our hearts.

PRAYER: *O Thou Ineffable One, I bow my head in awe at the thought of Thee, and lift up my mind and soul to be filled with the greatness that comes from Thee. Amen.*

131ST DAY

EFFORT BRINGS SUCCESS

When thou saidst, Seek ye my face; my heart said unto thee, Thy face, Lord, will I seek.   PSALM 27:8

Read PSALM 27:1-8

I have a friend who these forty years past has been practising through the understanding a realization of the Presence of God. To it he gives many other names; sometimes he calls it a simple *act*, or a clear and distinct *knowledge* of God; at other times, a *view* as through a glass, a loving *gaze*, an inward *sense* of God; yet again he terms it a *waiting* on God, a silent *converse* with Him, a *repose* in Him, the *life* and *peace* of the Soul. He says that by unweary efforts, by constantly recalling his mind to the Presence of God, a habit has been formed within him. . . . This intercourse with God he holds *in the depth of his being*; there it is that the soul speaks to God, heart to heart, and over the soul thus holding converse there steals a great and profound peace. All that passes without concerns the soul no more than a fire of straw, which the more it flares, the sooner burns itself out.

PRAYER: *O Lord, enlarge the chambers of my heart that I may find room for thy love. Sustain me by thy power, lest the fire of thy love consume me. Amen.*

132ND DAY

A STRAW FOR THE LOVE OF GOD

. . . that the word of the Lord may have free course, and be glorified.   II THESSALONIANS 3:1

Read II THESSALONIANS 3:1-5

I am giving you a picture of a lay-brother serving in a kitchen; let me then use his own words: "Nor is it needful that we should have great things to do. We can do *little* things for God; I turn the cake that is frying on the pan for love of Him, and that done, if there is nothing else to call me, I prostrate myself in worship before Him, who has given me grace to work; afterwards I am happier than a king. It is enough for me to pick up but a straw from the ground for the love of God."

PRAYER: *Holy Spirit of God, be in me today and all the while for the working out of thy purposes through me, and in me, and for me: and to God be glory forever. Amen.*

133RD DAY

ALWAYS WITH GOD

And Enoch walked with God: and he was not; for God took him.   GENESIS 5:24

Read GENESIS 5:21-24

The pious man is possessed by his awareness of the presence and nearness of God. Everywhere and at all times he lives as in His sight, whether he remains always heedful of His proximity or not. He feels embraced by God's mercy as by a vast encircling space. Awareness of God is as close to him as the throbbing of his own heart, often deep and calm but at times overwhelming, intoxicating, setting the soul afire. The momentous reality of God stands there as peace, power, and endless tranquility, as an inexhaustible source of help, as boundless compassion, as an open gate awaiting prayer.

It sometimes happens that the life of a pious man becomes so involved in God that his heart overflows as though it were a cup in the hand of God. This presence of God is not like the proximity of a mountain or the vicinity of an ocean, the view of which one may relinquish by closing the eyes or removing from the place. Rather is this convergence with God unavoidable, inescapable; like air in space, it is always being breathed in, even though one is not always aware of continuous respiration.

PRAYER: *Realization, O my God, more realization of the stupendous fact is what I ask for. In the name of Jesus Christ. Amen.*

134TH DAY

LOVE CAUSED THE REVELATION

The God of love and peace shall be with you. II CORINTHIANS 13:11

Read II CORINTHIANS 13:5-14

And from that time that [the revelation that had come to her] was shewed I desired oftentimes to witten what was our Lord's meaning. And fifteen years after, and more, I was answered in ghostly understanding, saying thus: "Wouldst thou witten thy Lord's meaning in this thing? Wit it well: Love was his meaning. Who shewed it thee? Love. What shewed He thee? Love. Wherefore shewed it He? For love. Hold thee therein and thou shalt witten and know more in the same. But thou shalt never know nor witten therein other thing without end." Thus was I learned that Love was our Lord's meaning. And I saw fully surely in this and in all, that ere God made us He loved us; which love was never slacked, nor ever shall be. And in this love He hath done all his works; and in this love He hath made all things profitable to us; and in this love our life is everlasting.

PRAYER: *Holy, holy, holy, Lord God Almighty. Glory be to Thee, who art everlasting Love. Pour into me, I pray, thy nature of outreaching, all-enfolding love. In the name of Jesus Christ. Amen.*

135TH DAY

THE PRIMAL THOUGHT

Hear, and your soul shall live.   ISAIAH 55:3

Read ISAIAH 55:1-3

Lift up thine heart unto God with a meek stirring of love; and mean Himself, and none of his goods. So that nought work in thy wit, nor in thy will, but only Himself. This is the work of the soul that most pleaseth God. For although it be good to think upon the kindness of God, and to love Him and praise Him for it, yet it is far better to think upon the naked being of Him, and to love Him and praise Him for Himself.

PRAYER: *O God, my God, Thou whom I need above all things else, Thou apart from whom I have no real life at all, my soul thirsteth for Thee, my flesh longeth for Thee. Teach me to do thy will, for Thou art my God. Cause me to know the way wherein I should walk, for I lift up my soul unto Thee. Help me in my effort to think of Thee, and to know Thee as I need to know Thee. To Thee be glory. Amen.*

136TH DAY

MY BEING DEPENDS ON GOD

All my springs are in thee.   PSALM 87:7

Read PSALM 87

There is an agent in my soul which is perfectly sensitive to God. I am as sure of this as I am that I am alive: nothing is as near to me as God is. My being depends on God's intimate presence. So, too, he is near to a stick or a stone but they do not know it. For that reason, a person may be more blessed than a stick, in that he recognizes God and knows how near he is. And the more he knows it, the more blessed he is; the less he knows it, the less his blessing. Man is not blessed because God is in him and so near that he *has* God—but that he is aware of how near God is, and knowing God, he loves Him.

O Thou Infinite and Eternal, I have partial awareness of Thee and some degree of communion with Thee: help me, I pray, to more awareness and deeper communion. In the name of Jesus Christ. Amen.

137TH DAY

LIGHT WITHOUT LOVE IS NOTHING

The darkness is passed, and the true light now shineth.   1 JOHN 2:8

Read 1 JOHN 2:7-11

Some may ask, "What is it to be 'a partaker of the divine nature,' or a Godlike man?" Answer: he who is imbued with or illuminated by the Eternal or divine Light, and inflamed or consumed with Eternal or divine love, he is a Godlike man and a partaker of the divine nature. . . . But ye must know that this Light or knowledge is worth nothing without Love. It is indeed true that Love must be guided and taught of Knowledge, but if Knowledge be not followed by Love, it will avail nothing. Let a man know much about God and divine things, nay, dream that he seeth and understandeth what God Himself is, if he have not Love, he will never become like unto God, or a "partaker of the divine nature." But if there be true Love along with his knowledge, he cannot but cleave to God, and forsake all that is not God or of Him.

PRAYER: *Save me, O my God, from all negligence and cowardice, and from all treachery of an unfaithful heart; and help me to find my way safely into thy haven. Amen.*

138TH DAY

INCREASING CAPACITY

Whosoever hath, to him shall be given, and he shall have more abundance.   MATTHEW 13:12

Read MATTHEW 13:1-12

A vessel that grows as it is filled will never be full. If a bin able to hold a cartload grew while you were dumping your load in it, you could never fill it. The soul is like that: the more it wants the more it is given; the more it receives the more it grows.

PRAYER: *Help me day by day to grow: to grow in the capacity for holding more of Thee, to increase in the receiving of Thee, to develop in the expression of Thee. In the name of Jesus Christ. Amen.*

THE ESSENCE OF IT

And Abraham fell on his face: and God talked with him. GENESIS 17:3

Read GENESIS 17:1-7

There is a characteristic type of religion, recognizable in all the great religions of the world, which may well be called mystical devotion. The essential characteristic of it is the attainment of personal conviction by an individual that the human spirit and the divine Spirit have met, have found each other, and are in mutual and reciprocal correspondence as spirit with Spirit. In short, mystical devotion means direct first-hand fellowship with God, and the deepened life-results which emerge. And this attitude of faith may rise, as it does with me in my best and sanest moments, to a joyous consciousness of acquaintance, fellowship, and love. Sometimes it is a flash of sudden insight, sometimes it is a quiet assurance, sometimes it is an unspeakable joy in living, sometimes it is a dim awareness of a resource to live by and to draw upon for action.

PRAYER: *Be Thou, O Lord, my protection. Direct my mind by thy gracious presence, and watch over my path with guiding love, that among the snares which lie hidden in this path wherein I walk, I may so pass onward with a heart fixed on Thee that I may come to be where Thou wouldst have me. Amen.*

OUR EXISTENCE MUST BE EXALTED

We would be . . . clothed upon, that mortality might be swallowed up of life. II CORINTHIANS 5:4

Read II CORINTHIANS 5:1-10

The greatest problem is not how to continue but how to exalt our existence. The cry for a life beyond the grave is presumptuous, if there is no cry for eternal life prior to our descending to the grave. Eternity is not perpetual future but perpetual presence. He has planted in us the seed of eternal life. The world to come is not only a hereafter but also a *herenow*. . . . This is the meaning of existence: to reconcile liberty with service, the passing with the lasting, to weave the threads of temporality into the fabric of eternity.

PRAYER: *Blessed art Thou, O Lord, who lightenest mine eyes, lest I sleep the sleep of death. Into thine hands I commit my spirit, soul, and body, which Thou hast created, redeemed, regenerated, O Lord, Thou God of truth; and together with me all mine and all that belongs to me. Preserve us from all evil, preserve our souls, I beseech Thee, O Lord. Keep us from falling, and present us faultless in the presence of thy glory in that day. And to Thee be praise forever. Amen.*

LOVE GOODNESS AS GOODNESS

Blessed be the God and Father of our Lord Jesus Christ, who hath blessed us with all spiritual blessings . . . in Christ. EPHESIANS 1:3

Read EPHESIANS 1:1-10

Now, wherever a man hath been made a partaker of the divine nature, in him is fulfilled the best and noblest life, and the worthiest in God's eyes, that hath been or can be. And of that eternal love which loveth Goodness as Goodness and for the sake of Goodness, a true, noble, Christ-like life is so greatly beloved, that it will never be forsaken or cast off. Where a man hath tasted this life, it is impossible for him ever to part with it, were he to live until the Judgment Day. And though he must die a thousand deaths, and though all the sufferings that ever befell all creatures could be heaped upon him, he would rather undergo them all, than fall away from this excellent life; and if he could exchange it for an angel's life, he would not.

PRAYER: *Into the faithful hands of the Eternal God I commit myself and my loved ones now and always. O my God, let me be thine and remain thine forever. Through Jesus Christ, thy Son. Amen.*

A STATE OF UNWORDED PRAYER

Set your affection on things above.   COLOSSIANS 3:2

Read COLOSSIANS 3:1-3

There is a way of life so hid with Christ in God that in the midst of the day's business one is inwardly lifting brief prayers, short ejaculations of praise, subdued whispers of adoration and of tender love to the Beyond that is within. No one need know about it. One can live in a well-nigh continuous state of unworded prayer, directed toward God, directed toward people and enterprises we have on our heart. There is no hurry about it all; it is a life unspeakable and full of glory, an inner world of splendor within which we, unworthy, may live. Some of you know it and live in it; others of you may wistfully long for it; it can be yours.

PRAYER: *Praise waiteth for Thee, O God, in Sion, and unto Thee shall the vow be performed. Thou art worthy, O Lord our God, the Holy One, to receive glory, and honour, and power. O Thou that hearest prayer, unto Thee shall all flesh come, shall my flesh come. O Lord, open Thou my lips, and my mouth shall shew forth thy praise. My soul doth praise the Lord for thy mercies towards myself, for all benefits received, for all successes, now or heretofore, for any good thing done. Glory be to Thee, Lord, and glory to thine all-holy name. Amen.*

LIVE WITH GREAT WORDS

I am the first, and I am the last; and beside me there is no God.   ISAIAH 44:6

Read ISAIAH 44:1-6

What time thou feelest by grace that thou art called of God, lift then up thine heart unto God with a meek stirring of love; and mean God that made thee, and bought thee, and that graciously hath called thee to thy degree, and receive none other thought of God. And yet not all these, but if thou list; for it sufficeth enough, a naked intent direct unto God without any other cause than Himself. And if thee list have this intent lapped and folden in one word, take thee but a little word of one syllable: for so it is better than of two, for ever the shorter it is the better it accordeth with the work of the Spirit. And such a word is this word GOD or this word LOVE. Choose thee whether thou wilt, or another; as thee list, which that thee liketh best of one syllable. And fasten this word to thine heart, so that it never go thence for thing that befalleth.

PRAYER: *My God! my God! my God! Help me to live in consciousness of Thee at all times, and to show forth thy Spirit in all my doings. Amen.*

TRUE POSSESSION OF GOD

My God shall be my strength.   ISAIAH 49:5

Read ISAIAH 49:1-6

Of what does this true possession of God consist, when one really has Him? It depends on the heart and an inner, intellectual return to God and not on steady contemplation by a given method. . . . We ought not to have or let ourselves be satisfied with the God we have thought of, for when the thought slips the mind, that God slips with it. What we want is rather the reality of God, exalted far above any human thought or creature. Then God will not vanish unless one turns away from him of his own accord. . . . Everything will taste like God and reflect him. God will shine in him all the time. . . . He will be like one athirst with a real thirst; he cannot help drinking even though he thinks of other things. . . . And the greater the thirst the more lively, deep-seated, present, and steady the idea of the Drink will be. . . . To be sure, this requires effort and love, a careful cultivation of the spiritual life, and a watchful, honest, active oversight of all one's mental attitudes toward things and people.

PRAYER: *I pray Thee, O Lord my God, teach me how to cultivate my spiritual life as it needs to be cultivated. In the name of Jesus Christ. Amen.*

KNOW THAT GOD IS

Thou art worthy, O Lord, to receive glory and honour and power: for thou hast created all things, and for thy pleasure they are and were created.
REVELATION 4:11

Read REVELATION 4:1-11

He truly knows God perfectly that feels Him incomprehensible and unable to be known. Thou askest what God is? I answer shortly to thee: such a one and so great is He that none other is or ever may be of like kind. If thou wilt know properly to speak what God is, I say thou shalt never find an answer to this question. I have not known; angels know not; archangels have not heard. Wot thou well God alone knows Himself, and may know. It is enough for thee therefore to know that God is. Also it is to be praised to know God perfectly; that is to say, He being unable to be fully conceived: knowing Him to love Him; loving Him to sing in Him; singing to rest in Him, and by inward rest to come to endless rest. God is to be loved, to be praised, to be worshipped and glorified, the only Maker of all things; above all things; through all things, and in all things: that is blessed in the world of worlds. Amen.

PRAYER: *Hail therefore O lovely Everlasting Love! Come into me, my Beloved! Amen.*

WHAT DISPLEASES GOD

Better it is to be of an humble spirit with the lowly, than to divide the spoil with the proud.   PROVERBS 16:19

Read PROVERBS 16:18-22

God is more displeased with a proud righteous man than a meek sinner. . . . Truly this meekness gives praise to Christ, noy [*sic*] to the fiend, and joy to God's people; it makes Christ's servant to love more burningly, to serve more devoutly, to praise more worthily; and makes him fuller of charity. The more that a man meeks himself the more he raises God's worship on high. He that truly perseveres in the love of God and of his neighbour, and yet thinks himself unworthier and lower than others, by meekness and knowledge of himself overcomes enemies, and conquers the love of the High Judge, and shall be received into endless joy when he passes from this light.

PRAYER: *O God, who hast taught us that we are most truly free when we find our wills in thine; help me to gain this liberty by continual surrender unto Thee, that I may walk in the way which Thou hast ordained for me and in doing thy will may find my life. Through Jesus Christ. Amen.*

WHERE IS REST TO BE FOUND?

Return unto thy rest, O my soul.   PSALM 116:7

Read PSALM 116:1-9

If ever there was a question which it concerns us all to answer it is this, Where is rest to be found? There is no rest for the heart of man save in God. But how shall we rest in God? By giving ourselves wholly to Him. If you give yourself by halves, you cannot find full rest; and for this reason it is that so few Christians attain to a full, stedfast, unchanging peace—they do not seek rest in God only, or give themselves up to Him without reserve. True rest is secret, abundant, without a regret or a wish. It stills all passion, restrains the imagination, steadies the mind, controls all wavering. A countless host of God's faithful servants have drunk deeply of it amid the daily burden of a weary life—dull, commonplace, painful, or desolate. All that God has been to them He is ready to be to you.

PRAYER: *Help me, O my God, help me to find my way into thy Centre of Stillness, and to realize that it is only harmony with Thee that can give rest to my soul. In the name of Jesus Christ, the Light of the world. Amen.*

THE MOST HIGH NATURE OF GOD

Who shall not fear thee, O Lord, and glorify thy name? for thou only art holy. REVELATION 15:4

Read REVELATION 15:2-4

The most high nature of the Godhead may thus be perceived and beheld: how it is Simplicity and Onefoldness, inaccessible Height and bottomless Depth, incomprehensible Breadth and eternal Length, a dark Silence, a wild Desert, the Rest of all saints in the Unity, and a common Fruition of Himself and of all saints in Eternity. And many other marvels may be seen in the abysmal Sea of the Godhead; and though, because of the senses to which they must be shown from without, we must use sensible images, yet, in truth, these things are perceived and beheld from within, as an abysmal and unconditioned Good. The enlightened man shall also mark and behold the attributes of the Father in the Godhead: how He is omnipotent power and Might, Creator, Mover, Preserver, Beginning and End, the Origin and Being of all creatures.

PRAYER: *O thou Ineffable One, I bow my head in awe at the thought of Thee, and lift up my mind and soul to be filled with greatness that comes from Thee. Amen.*

WHAT IS IT TO BE SAVED?

My heart is fixed, O God, my heart is fixed.   PSALM
57:7

Read PSALM 57:7-11

Do not all Christians desire to have Christ to be
their Saviour? Yes. But here is the deceit; all would
have Christ to be their Saviour in the *next* world
and to help them into Heaven when they die by
his power and merits with God. But this is not
willing Christ to be thy Saviour; for his salvation, if
it is had, must be had in *this* world; if He saves thee
it must be done in this life, by changing and alter-
ing all that is within thee, by helping thee to a
new heart. . . . For to have salvation from Christ
is nothing else but to be made like unto Him; it is to
have his humility and meekness, his mortification
and self-denial, his renunciation of the spirit, wisdom, and honours of this world, his love of God,
his desire of doing God's will and seeking only his
honour.

PRAYER: *O God, whose blessed Son came not to
do His own will but thine alone, open my heart
to every call from Thee, my mind to every thought
that would advance me in thy salvation. Keep me,
I pray, from failing Thee at any time. In the name
of Jesus Christ. Amen.*

LOVE GOD FOR HIMSELF

The Lord hath appeared of old unto me, saying,
Yea, I have loved thee with an everlasting love:
therefore with lovingkindness have I drawn thee.
JEREMIAH 31:3

Read JEREMIAH 31:1-3

Although it be good to think upon the kindness
of God, and to love Him and praise Him for it, yet
it is far better to think upon the naked being of
Him, and to love Him and praise Him for Himself.
But now thou askest me and sayest, "How shall I
think on Himself, and what is He?" and to this I
cannot answer thee but this: "I wot not." For of all
other creatures and their works, yea, and of the
works of God's self, may a man through grace have
fullhead of knowing, but of God Himself can no
man think. And therefore I would leave all that
thing that I can think, and choose to my love that
thing that I cannot think. For why; He may well
be loved, but not thought. By love may He be
gotten and holden; but by thought never.

PRAYER: *Every day will I bless Thee, my God,
by whom all things were made, in heaven and in
earth, visible and invisible; who hast not suffered
my heart to be hardened, but hast left me com-
punction of soul. O my God, though I know not
how to think of Thee, yet I can love Thee; and I do
love Thee, and would have my love grow ever
greater and truer. Amen.*

GOD FILLS HEAVEN AND EARTH

Can any hide himself in secret places that I shall not see him? saith the Lord. Do not I fill heaven and earth? saith the Lord.   JEREMIAH 23:24

Read JEREMIAH 23:24-29

Highly ought we to rejoice that God dwelleth in our soul, and much more highly ought we to rejoice that our soul dwelleth in God. Our soul is made to be God's dwelling place; and the dwelling place of the soul is God. . . . And high understanding it is, inwardly to see and know that God, which is our Maker, dwelleth in our soul; and an higher understanding it is, inwardly to see and to know that our soul, that is made, dwelleth in God's substance: of which substance, God, we are that we are. . . . Mine understanding took that our Substance is in God: that is to say, that God is God, and our Substance is a creature in God. For the Almighty Truth of the Trinity is our Father: for he made us and keepeth us in him.

PRAYER: *O my God, kindle in me, to thy glory, I pray, the flame of thy indwelling Presence, and make my life to be as a very fire going forth from Thee into the world. In the name of Jesus Christ. Amen.*

INTENTION AND LOVE FIND GOD

Canst thou by searching find out God? canst thou find out the Almighty unto perfection? JOB 11:7

Read JOB 9:1-11

This is the highest knowledge of God which any man may have in the active life: that he should confess in the light of faith that God is incomprehensible and unknowable. . . . But where intelligence remains without, desire and love go in. When the soul is thus stretched towards God, by intention and by love, above everything that it can understand, then it rests and dwells in God, and God in it. When the soul climbs with desire above the multiplicity of creatures, and above the works of the senses, and above the light of nature, then it meets Christ in the life of faith. When it stretches itself with longing towards this incomprehensible God, then it meets Christ, and is filled with his gifts. And when it loves and rests above all gifts, and above itself, and above all creatures, then it dwells in God, and God dwells in it.

PRAYER: *My God! my God! who art eternal Mystery but also Light Everlasting, shine in my heart I pray, shine through my life I pray, so that I may help to give the light of the knowledge of the glory of God in the face of Christ Jesus at all times, wherever I may be, to all people. And to Thee and Christ Jesus be glory. Amen.*

ALL ONE IN GOD

They shall come from the east, and from the west, and from the north and from the south, and shall sit down in the kingdom of God. LUKE 13:29

Read LUKE 13:22-30

There is only one source of Life—an Infinite and Almighty Life, whose creative power gave life to all living things. All creatures live in Him, and in Him will they remain forever. Again this Life created innumerable other lives, and in the stages of their progress man is one of these, created in God's own image that he might ever remain happy in His holy presence. This life may change but it can never be destroyed, and though the change from one form of existence to another is called Death, this never means that death finally ends life. It merely transfers the life from one form of existence to another.

PRAYER: *Lord, my God, great, eternal, wonderful in glory, who keepest covenant and promises for those that love Thee with their whole heart, who art the Life of all, the Help of those that flee unto Thee, the Hope of those who cry unto Thee, cleanse me body and soul, heart and conscience, that with a pure heart and a clear soul, with perfect love and calm hope, I may venture confidently and fearlessly to go through life this day and every day. In the name of Jesus Christ. Amen.*

EITHER HELL OR HEAVEN GROWS

Abound more and more.   1 THESSALONIANS 4:1

Read 1 THESSALONIANS 3:11-4:1

God is, must be, the one flawless Home of the Soul, where the only surprise is the wanderer's desire to be elsewhere. He is supremely natural for us. So it is natural that Hell and Heaven should be here; because we are changing, and where we are these must be, our states and places matching us within and without, and each growing more and more clear to us as we grow more and more clear to ourselves. For each man and woman among us it is either Hell or Heaven that grows; and either darkness or light increases in Earth. The kingdom of Heaven is within us, so is the kingdom of Hell. I have my choice in consenting to determine in one fashion rather than in another the world to which I go and the body which shall rise with me, and I make choice by the turning of my heart this side or that.

PRAYER: *Everlasting Savior, as moment by moment I have to choose what to let myself think, and how to let myself feel and react, and what to say and do, help me, I pray, so that at all times and in all things I shall manifest the presence of thy Spirit within me. In the name of Jesus Christ. Amen.*

TO REACH ASSURANCE

He which hath begun a good work in you will perform it.   PHILIPPIANS 1:6

Read PHILIPPIANS 1:1-9

He Who is Infinite, Perfect, Holy—the Source of all holiness—you are bound to Him by every possible tie and gift in the past and present, by every hope of the future. . . . We must not measure the reality of love by feelings, but by results. Feelings are very delusive. They often depend upon mere natural temperament. A glowing imagination is apt to seek self rather than God. But if you persevere amid temptation, dryness, weariness, and desolation, you may rest assured that your love is real. As men advance in the interior life, they learn to indulge less and less in self-dissection, even as regards their love of God—and this is the higher and purer form of love. It is free from all self-complacency, absorbed in God Himself.

PRAYER: *Almighty God, lead me, thy child, into such a consciousness of thy ever-nearness and thy all-enfolding love that I shall live at all times in utter confidence in Thee. In the name of Jesus Christ. Amen.*

WATCH FOR GOD EVERYWHERE

Watch ye therefore: for ye know not when the master of the house cometh.   MARK 13:35

Read MARK 13:28-37

In all his work, and on every occasion, a man should make clear use of his reason and have a conscious insight into himself and his spirituality and distinguish God to the highest possible degree in everything. One should be, as our Lord said, "Like people always on the watch, expecting their Lord." Expectant people are watchful, always looking for Him they expect, always ready to find Him in whatever comes along; however strange it may be, they always think He might be in it. The man to whom God is ever present, and who controls and uses his mind to the highest degree—that man alone knows what peace is and he has the Kingdom of Heaven within him.

PRAYER: *My God! my God! my God! Above all things else I need Thee, and above all things else I desire Thee. Help me to recognize Thee wherever thy Presence is to be found, and to be very responsive to Thee at all times. In the name of the Eternal Helper. Amen.*

THE SOUL'S LIFE AND FOOD

Unto the upright there ariseth light in the darkness. PSALM 112:4

Read PSALM 112:1-7

Prayer is an intercourse of the soul with God. It is the medium through which life and food are conveyed to the soul. Every secret aspiration of the soul to God is prayer. The simple and undisguised emotions of filial love are infinitely more expressive than the most studied language. The spirit of God needs none of our arrangements and methods. To teach man to seek God in his heart, to think of Him, to return to Him whenever he finds he has wandered from Him, and to do and suffer all things with a single eye to please Him, is the natural and ready process; it is leading the soul to the very source of Grace.

PRAYER: *O Thou Infinite and Eternal, Everlasting Father, speak to me, I pray. Give me the instructions I need for this day. In the name of Jesus Christ. Amen.*

IF I LIVE IN GOD'S PRESENCE

Though I walk in the midst of trouble, thou wilt revive me.   PSALM 138:7

Read PSALM 138

The effects of the blessed, perceptible presence of God in perfect souls are unspeakable and divine; for He is in them both as a principle of all their actions internal and external, being the life of their life and spirit of their spirits; and also as the end of them, directing both the actions and persons to Himself only. He is all in all things unto them: a light to direct securely all their steps, and to order all their workings, even those also which seem the most indifferent, the which by the guidance of God's Holy Spirit do cause a farther advancement of them to a yet more immediate union. He is a shield to protect them in all temptations and dangers, an internal force and vigour within them, to make them do and suffer all things whatsoever his pleasure is they should do or suffer. They not only believe and know, but even feel and taste Him to be the universal, infinite Good.

PRAYER: *Choose, I beseech Thee, my heart for thy dwelling-place, Thou Infinite and Eternal; adorn it, replenish it with spiritual gifts, and wholly possess it. And to Thee be glory forever. Amen.*

WHEN LIGHT FAILS TO COME

Mine eyes are unto thee, O God the Lord: in thee is my trust. PSALM 141:8

Read ACTS 1:15-26

Now if it should happen that, after trials by prayer made for the knowing of the divine will, the soul should yet perceive no sufficient light, nor any considerable inclination, propension, or preponderation towards one side more than another, in this case she may freely and confidently, as it were by lots, make choice indifferently of whether she thinks fit; and a choice so made, whenever it happens, she may and ought to believe to be according to God's will, since, having done her part to know His will, after all this is the result of her recollections, in which she has to her utmost power carried herself with resignation and indifference.

PRAYER: *To Thee, my God and Savior, I commend my soul, my body, my seeing, my hearing, taste, smell, and touching; all my cogitations, affections, words, and actions; my sense and understanding; my memory, faith, and belief; and my constancy in well-doing; all these I commend into the hands of thy powerful protection, to the end that all the nights and days, hours and moments of my life, Thou mayest preserve and direct me. Praise to Thee, O Lord my God! Amen.*

WHAT LOVE LEADS TO

Above all things have fervent charity [love]. I PETER 4:8

Read I PETER 4:7-11

Nothing exalts, nothing purifies but the fire of love; nothing changes death into life, earth into Heaven, men into angels but love alone. Love breathes the Spirit of God; its words and works are the inspiration of God. It speaketh not of itself, but the Word, the eternal Word of God speaketh in it; for all that love speaketh, that God speaketh, because love is God. Love is Heaven revealed in the soul; it is light and truth. It lives in the liberty, the universality, the impartiality of Heaven. It has no by-ends; it seeks not its own; it has but one will, and that is to give itself into everything and overcome all evil with good. It comes down from Heaven; it regenerates the soul from above. Its meat and drink is to do the will of God.

PRAYER: *My God, my God, Thou hast taught us that love is the one greatest and first law of life. Kindle in me, O kindle in me, the divine fire which transforms into thy likeness the soul in which it burns, and makes that soul a saving power in the world. And to Thee be glory. Amen.*

FIND GOD THROUGH LOVE

I have loved thee with an everlasting love.
JEREMIAH 31:3

Read JEREMIAH 31:1-3

Love may reach to God in this life, but not knowing. And, therefore, if thou wilt stand and not fall,
cease never in thine intent: but beat evermore on
this cloud of unknowing that is betwixt thee and
thy God with a sharp dart of longing love. Fast
thou never so much, wake thou never so early; yea,
and if it were lawful to do—as it is not—put thou
out thine eyes, cut thou out thy tongue of thy
mouth, stop thou thine ears and thy nose never so
fast, do all the pain to thy body that thou mayest
or canst think: all this would help thee right nought.
For virtue is nought else but an ordained and a
measured affection, plainly directed unto God for
himself.

PRAYER: *O God, who hast prepared for those
who love Thee such good things as pass man's understanding, I would love Thee not for thy promises
alone, but for Thyself. In the name of Jesus Christ.
Amen.*

IS HE NOT ALMIGHTY?

Having his Father's name written in their foreheads.
REVELATION 14:1

Read REVELATION 14:1-5

Though the world, the flesh and the enemy, the fiend, and the four elements, the birds of the air and the beasts of the earth tormented [the soul] and despised her and devoured her, if it might so be, what might she lose, if God dwelled with her? Oh, is He not Almighty? Yes, without doubt, He is all might, all wisdom, and all goodness: our Father, our brother and our true friend; He is without beginning and shall be without ending, He is without comprehending but of Himself, and without end was, is, and shall be, three persons and one God only. "Such is the Beloved of our souls," saith this soul.

PRAYER: *Father of lights, from whose unshadowed home above comes every good and every perfect gift, I receive as from thy hand my share in the common blessings which, without respect of persons, hourly descend upon mankind. I thank Thee for the special tokens of thy friendship and personal care that have made me glad. Help me to use these and all thy bounties according to thy design, that my whole life may be a hymn of praise to Thee. Through Jesus Christ, our Lord. Amen.*

HE KNOCKS AT THE DOOR

If any man hear my voice, and open the door, I will come in to him. REVELATION 3:20

Read REVELATION 3:14-21

I would not turn my own thoughts or call the attention of Christians to anything but the one thing needful. If it be asked what this one thing is, it is the Spirit of God brought again to his first power of life in us. Nothing else is wanted by us. Everything else, be it what it will, however glorious and divine in outward appearance, is dead and helpless, but so far as it is the immediate work of the Spirit of God breathing and living in it. "Ye are not in the flesh," says the Apostle, "but in the spirit"; but then he adds, as the only ground of this, "if so be that the spirit of God dwelleth in you"; surely he means, if so be ye are moved, guided, and governed by that which the Spirit wills, works, and inspires within you.

PRAYER: *Thou knowest my need, my daily need, my momentary need, O Lord, my God: grant therefore, I pray, according to the riches of thy glory, that I may be strengthened with power through thy Spirit in the inward man, and that Christ may dwell in my heart through faith continually. And unto Thee be glory forever. Amen.*

LOVE ALWAYS ACTIVE

Wait on the Lord; yea, wait, I say, on the Lord.
PSALM 27:14

Read PSALM 27:8-14

A son who loves his father does not always think distinctly of him; many objects draw away his mind, but these never interrupt the filial love; whenever his father returns into his thoughts, he loves him, and he feels, in the very inmost of his heart, that he has never discontinued one moment to love him, though he has ceased to think of him. In this manner should we love our heavenly Father. . . . True religion is a heaven-born thing; it is an emanation of the truth and goodness of God upon the spirits of men, whereby they are formed into a similitude and likeness of himself, and become "partakers of the Divine nature."

PRAYER: *O my God, take my mind and think through it, take my lips and speak through them, take my heart and set it on fire with thy wisdom and love, take my strength and use it to do thy work in the world; and let this be so at all times, whether I am consciously thinking of Thee or not. In the name of Jesus Christ. Amen.*

NOT SEEN, YET SEEN

The invisible things of him from the creation of the world are clearly seen, being understood by the things that are made, even his eternal power and Godhead. ROMANS 1:20

Read ROMANS 1:14-20

Of these intellectual passive unions, the supreme and most noble that may be had in this life is that whereby God is contemplated without any perceptible images, by a certain intellectual supernatural light darted into the soul; for herein though God be not seen as He is, yet He is clearly seen that He is, and that He is incomprehensible. Mystic authors call this a divine passive union; a union exercised more by the will than the understanding, although the effect thereof be to refund great light into the understanding.

PRAYER: *Holy, Holy, Holy, Lord God of Sabaoth; heaven and earth are full of the majesty of thy glory. O my God, my helper, I will hope in Thee; thy mercy is in heaven, and thy truth reacheth to the clouds. Thy kingdom is a kingdom forever, and thy reign is for all generations. My Beloved is mine, and I am his. Amen.*

CLAD IN THE GOODNESS OF GOD

I will greatly rejoice in the Lord, my soul shall be joyful in my God; for he hath clothed me with the garments of salvation.   ISAIAH 61:10

Read ISAIAH 61:10, 11

As the body is clad in the cloth, and the flesh in the skin, and the bones in the flesh, and the heart in the whole, so are we, soul and body, clad in the Goodness of God, and enclosed. Yea, and more homely—for all these may waste and wear away, but the Goodness of God is ever whole—and more near to us, without any likeness; for truly our Lover desireth that our soul cleave to Him with all its might, and that we be evermore cleaving to his Goodness. . . . For our kindly will is to have God, and the Good Will of God is to have us; and we may never cease from willing nor from longing, till we have Him in fullness of joy.

PRAYER: *O Lord, my God, who callest upon thy children to be perfect even as Thou art perfect, so encompass me with thy completeness that I may be able to rise up out of my incompleteness, my littleness, my pettiness, and all that is contrary to Thee and to make each day a truer and stronger manifestation of thy Goodness. By the help of Jesus Christ. Amen.*

SELF? OR GOD?

For as the heavens are higher than the earth, so are my ways higher than your ways, and my thoughts than your thoughts.   ISAIAH 55:9

Read ISAIAH 55:6-9

Above all, He requires self-renunciation in all things and for ever. . . . True self-renunciation leaves all the future to God, and only seeks to do its plain duty at the present moment. God does not require of us any of those glowing religious emotions which are too often a subtle food to self-love. All such gifts are his alone, He can give and recall them as He sees fit; therefore do not be troubled when you are dry, dull, unable to rouse yourself to any holy thoughts in prayer or communion—still less must you fancy that such prayers and communion are worthless. [God] does not require us to have so absolute a control over our imagination as wholly to rule our thoughts. That is beyond our power, but it is within our power not to dwell upon distracting thoughts. As to what we should ask of God—above all, we must ask a true knowledge of God and of ourselves; [and belief] in Him unquestioning, undoubting, through whatever darkness or trial may come upon us.

PRAYER: *Help me, O Thou Infinite and Eternal, ever more clearly to know thy ways and to do them. In the name of Jesus Christ. Amen.*

THE OCEAN OF GOD'S PRESENCE

One God and Father of all, who is above all, and through all, and in you all.   EPHESIANS 4:6

Read EPHESIANS 4:1-16

As the sea is full of water, so is the whole universe filled with God. When one dives under water, above and below and round about there is nothing but water. And just as in the water of the sea there are uncounted living creatures, so in the Infinite Being of God his creatures exist. In this world of spirits the spiritual progress of anyone governs the degree to which he is able to know and feel God. God's presence can indeed be felt and enjoyed, but it cannot be expressed in words. As the sweetness of the sweet is enjoyed by tasting, and not by the most graphic descriptive phrasing, so everyone in heaven experiences the joy of God's presence, and everyone in the spiritual world knows that his experience of God is real.

PRAYER: *O Lord, my God, who art Life, and Love, and Light, and Truth, and Wisdom, and Power; O Thou all-enfolding: help me, thy struggling servant, to realize that my being is involved in that immortal and eternal ocean of Life and Love and Light and Truth and Wisdom and Power, and help me to draw strength into myself continually from that realization. And to Thee be praise and glory forever. Amen.*

LIVE TO MANIFEST GOD'S GLORY

Unto the King eternal, immortal, invisible, the only wise God, be honour and glory for ever and ever. Amen.   I TIMOTHY 1:17

Read I TIMOTHY 1:15-17

In the Eternal Spirit, all things, all events, all beings have their place. The soul of man looks inward and beholds the subtle, elusive, mysterious, pervasive, all-containing God. He is the king immortal and invisible whom the eye of the soul may habitually behold. His presence in human existence is the source of all our standards of right, of all our measures of love, of all our experiences of power, of all our hopes of complete moral being. He provides room in his own life for all; He is the elusive and yet essential condition of all finite life. By the inspirations of the Almighty we exist and become self-conscious souls and men of understanding heart. The mystic faces the future undismayed and in serene confidence, and God is the ground of his hope.

PRAYER: *Heaven and earth are full of thy glory, O Thou Eternal God: work in my mind and soul by the power of thy Spirit, I pray, so that they also may manifest that glory. Amen.*

WE MUST CULTIVATE FAITH

According to your faith be it unto you.   MATTHEW
9:29

Read MATTHEW 9:27-31

Consider how was it that the lame and blind, the
lunatic and leper, the publican and sinner, found
Christ to be their Saviour and to do all that for
them which they wanted to be done to them? It was
because they had a real desire of having that which
they asked for, and therefore in true faith and
prayer applied to Christ, that his Spirit and power
might enter into them and heal that which they
wanted and desired to be healed in them. Every one
of these said in faith and desire, "Lord, if Thou wilt,
Thou canst make me whole." And the answer was
always this, "According to your faith, be it unto
you." . . . And here lies the whole reason of our
falling short of the salvation of Christ; it is because
we have no will to it.

PRAYER: *O living Christ, make me ever conscious
of Thy healing nearness. Touch my eyes that I may
see Thee in a right way; open the ears of my soul
that I may hear thy every speaking to me; help me
at all times to be conscious of Thee, and to partake
of thy strength, thy healing life, thy saving love.
Amen.*

GOD'S WILL OUR PEACE

These things I have spoken unto you, that in me ye might have peace.   JOHN 16:33

Read JOHN 16:25-33

Man has ever given way to God. Why then should I be afraid?

As the air is penetrated by the sun, thus we receive in peace the Incomprehensible Light, enfolding and penetrating us.

God's every infliction is a lure. I give no thanks to God for loving me because He cannot help it, it is his nature to; what I do thank Him for is that He cannot of his goodness leave off loving me.

PRAYER: *Eternal Father, in whose word it is said that if we will but lift up the gates and throw open the doors of our being the King of Glory will come in, help me to lift up the gates of my mind and heart and soul, and to afford Thee abundant entrance. I need Thee. My groping mind needs Thee. My hungry heart needs Thee. My laboring spirit needs Thee. I long for Thee. I long for more of Thee. I languish because I have not more of Thee. Help me to open myself utterly to Thee. I lift up my gates and doors. Come Thou, O King of Glory, come Thou in. Amen.*

WE NEED VISIONS OF GLORY

This was the appearance of the likeness of the glory of the Lord. And when I saw it, I fell upon my face, and I heard a voice of one that spake.   EZEKIEL 1:28

Read EZEKIEL 1:1-28

We have got to saturate ourselves with the rainbows and the sunset marvels in order to radiate them. It is as much our duty to live in the beauty of the presence of God on some mount of transfiguration until we become white with Christ as it is for us to go down where they grope, and grovel, and groan, and lift them to new life. After all the deepest truth is that the Christlike life is glorious, undefeatably glorious. There is no defeat unless one loses God, and then all is defeat though it be housed in castles and buried in fortunes.

PRAYER: *O Thou God of all grace, who hast called thy children to look up unto thy eternal glory, and to climb up unto fullness of life in that glory through Christ Jesus, I pray that Thou wilt perfect, stablish, strengthen, and settle me so that I shall never fall from the way but shall with increasing steadiness walk in the path which Thou hast ordained. I give myself to Thee, O Lord, my God. Amen.*

A SOUL'S CRY

O Lord, thou art my God; I will exalt thee, I will praise thy name.   ISAIAH 25:1

Read ISAIAH 25:1-9

O my soul, when wilt thou perfectly love thy God?

If thou hast sinned and art wounded, behold thy God, behold thy physician is ready to cure thee.

Love Him, then, love Him of whom thou art beloved; attend to Him that attendeth to thee, and seek Him that seeketh thee.

Love this Lover, of whom thou art beloved, with whose love thou art prevented, and who is the fountain from whence thy love floweth.

He hath promised those things unto thee, which neither eye hath seen, nor ear hath heard, nor can the heart of man comprehend.

Heaven and earth and all therein contained do continually exhort thee to love thy Lord God.

Let Him teach thee so to live as being always in his presence.

Let Him possess thy heart as his temple, and reign in it as his throne.

PRAYER: *Eternal Love, enter into my being and possess it. Dwell within me with the spirit of power and the deep peace of a triumphant hope, and help me to serve Thee in fruitfulness and joy. And when at last the day is done, and my work is ended, and the night falls, let the dimness of my evening be the dawn of thy eternal morning. In the name of Jesus Christ. Amen.*

174TH DAY

UNTIL CHRIST BE FORMED IN YOU

He that eateth of this bread shall live for ever.
JOHN 6:58

Read JOHN 6:41-58

To eat the body and blood of Christ is neither more nor less than to put on Christ, to receive birth and life and nourishment and growth from Him. When it is said that we must eat the flesh and blood of Christ, it is the same thing as saying that Christ must be formed in us, or manifested in us. You must therefore consider the sacrament purely as an object of your devotion that is to raise, exercise, and inflame every holy ardor of your soul that tends to God. As you can receive or believe nothing higher of our Savior than that He is a real principle of life to us, so every height and depth of devotion, faith, love, and adoration which is due to God as your Creator is due to God as your redeemer.

PRAYER: *Lord Christ, I am not worthy to receive Thee into myself, but I need Thee. I need Thee for the cleansing of my mind and soul; I need Thee for the forgiveness of my sins and for keeping me from further sin; I need Thee so that I may never be separated from Thee because of the sins that have stained my life but may live as thy true disciple every day and hour. To Thee, my Savior and Lord, be praise. Amen.*

175TH DAY

THE SOURCE OF COMFORT

As the sufferings of Christ abound in us, so our consolation also aboundeth by Christ. II CORIN-THIANS 1:5

Read II CORINTHIANS 1:1-5

If you go to prayer with the spirit and intention of praying, so long as you retract not that intention, although your thoughts may wander, you will, nevertheless, pray in spirit and in truth. Almighty Power, in due time, will help you to overcome all your difficulties. Distrust not Him, therefore, but only yourselves; and remember that, as the apostle saith, "He is the father of mercies, and God of all comforts." Be of good courage then, and though it may seem to you that you toil without gaining much advantage, yet you must recollect we must plough and sow before we can reap; and if you persevere in faith and patience, you will reap an abundant reward for all your labours.

PRAYER: *Grant, O Father, that as thy blessed Son did turn from much business to quiet communion with Thee, so I in life's strain and stress may find in Thee my strength and peace. Through Jesus Christ, my Lord. Amen.*

176TH DAY

GOD IS ALL LOVE

Strengthen ye the weak hands, and confirm the feeble knees. Say to them that are of a fearful heart, Be strong, fear not.   ISAIAH 35:3, 4

Read ISAIAH 35:1-10

Some people have a notion of the Christian religion as if God was thereby declared full of wrath against fallen man, that nothing but the blood of his only begotten Son could satisfy his vengeance. Nay, some have gone such lengths of wickedness as to assert that God had, by immutable decrees, reprobated and rejected a great part of the race of Adam to an inevitable damnation, to show forth and magnify the glory of his justice. But these are miserable mistakers of the divine nature. For God is love, yea, all love; and so all love, that nothing but love can come from Him. God has only one common nature of goodness towards all created nature, calling everything to the highest happiness it is capable of.

PRAYER: *My mouth shall speak the praise of the Lord. I will give thanks unto Thee, O Lord, with my whole heart. I will sing unto Thee, in the sight of the angels. Accept the praises which I desire to offer. Thou art my God, and I will praise Thee; I will sing unto the Lord as long as I live: I will sing praise to my God while I have my being. Amen: Alleluia. Hosanna in the highest.*

177TH DAY

THE SPIRIT ALSO NEEDS REST

Come ye yourselves apart into a desert place, and rest a while.   MARK 6:31

Read MARK 6:7-13, 30-33

The very effort to understand, to meditate, to consider different aspects of religion, to form some idea of the nature of Almighty God, may render the soul impervious to the direct action of the Holy Spirit. Rest is necessary for the soul as well as for the body; rest, in which the forces of grace refresh and recreate the soul. This rest cannot be obtained only by employing the soul in various spiritual activities. Just as the body needs sleep in order to recruit its energies, so does the soul require a silent resting in the Presence of God. For in this rest God will speak and the soul will hear.

PRAYER: *O my God, I rest myself in Thee. Thou, O Lord, my God, art my stay, and my strength, and my hope. Thy hands have made me and fashioned me. Through Thee have I been upheld through all my days, and my praise shall be always of Thee. Help me to live in awareness of Thee at all times, even as Jesus Christ, my great example, lived in continual awareness of Thee. Amen.*

178TH DAY

SOUL-LIFE MUST BE NOURISHED

And did all eat the same spiritual meat; and did all drink the same spiritual drink. 1 CORINTHIANS 10:3, 4

Read 1 CORINTHIANS 10:1-4

I am a babe; and I feed on life, the divine life brought to me as I am capable of absorbing it. My body-life is nourished by the bread of earth, and my soul-life is nourished by bread the angels share. I dare to say that I absorb the very life of God for the feeding of my life in body and soul. He must nourish me with Himself, or in soul and body I go down into the pit and shrink to my starved nothingness. There comes too with all these thoughts one of great joy—my soul can feed on Him unmediated save by Himself made Man in me, because He is so near, nearer than all my kin, near as my own self, and with greater love for me.

PRAYER: *O Lord, whose strength is made perfect in weakness, help me in my weakness to feel the mighty tides of thy Spirit pouring into me, so that I may not turn coward before life's challenges nor prove recreant to its duties. Amen.*

SELF-WILL MUST GO

Whosoever will save his life shall lose it: and whosoever will lose his life for my sake shall find it.
MATTHEW 16:25

Read MATTHEW 16:21-26

Nothing hath separated us from God but our own will, or rather our own will is our separation from God. All the disorder and corruption and malady of our nature lies in a certain fixedness of our own will, imagination, and desire, wherein we live to ourselves, are our own center and circumference, act wholly from ourselves, according to our own will, imagination, and desires. It is this self that our Saviour calls upon us to deny; it is this life of self that we are to hate and to lose, that the Kingdom of God may arise in us, that is, that God's will may be done in us. All other sacrifices that we make, whether of worldly goods, honours, or pleasures, are but small matters compared to that sacrifice and destruction of all selfishness, as well spiritual as natural.

PRAYER: *My God! my God! My God and my salvation, help me so to will and to do after thy good pleasure, help me to such faithfulness and steadfastness in thy service, that I may both be true to Thee myself and also may help others to find joy and rest in Thee. In the name of Jesus Christ. Amen.*

180TH DAY

EVERYTHING IS IMPORTANT

Every idle word that men shall speak, they shall give account thereof in the day of judgment. MATTHEW 12:36

Read MATTHEW 12:30-37

God is the great I Am; and within his eternal "Now" each of my passing moments has its place and an enduring meaning which is both his and mine. The least event of my life is held in his— one of the sparrows whose fall He knows. My history, my process, is the mutal act by which the divine life and the human are being made at one. Thus I, the impure, am embraced within the high and holy God who inhabiteth eternity. I am a work of art—and an artist—not a piece of mechanism being gradually improved to a static perfection. There is no least thing of which I dare to say "it does not matter." There is nothing hidden that shall not be revealed, because all things are significant;

and even for their "idle" words men must account, because there are no idle words.

PRAYER: *Come in, O Christ, and judge me; come and cast out from me every sin that hinders Thee; come and purge my soul by thy Presence. Come, and be my King, for ever and ever. Amen.*

181ST DAY

MY INWARD CRAVING IS FOR GOD

God so loved the world, that he gave his only be-gotten Son, that whosoever believeth in him should not perish, but have everlasting life.   JOHN 3:16

Read JOHN 3:16-21

As long as we inwardly perceive that God would be ours, the goodness of God touches our inward craving: and therefrom springs the wildness of love, for the touch which pours forth from God stirs up this wildness, and demands our activity, that is, that we should love eternal love. For all the rivers of the grace of God pour forth, and the more we taste of them, the more we long to taste; and the more we long to taste, the more deeply we press into contact with Him; and the more deeply we press into con-tact with God, the more the flood of his sweetness flows through us and over us; and the more we are thus drenched and flooded, the better we feel and know that the sweetness of God is incomprehensible and unfathomable.

PRAYER: *O Thou, Creator and Savior, so fill me with thy Spirit that the ears which have heard thy call shall be closed to all that is contrary to Thee; the eyes which have been lifted up to the vision of thy glory shall be continually fixed on the vision of Thee; the feet which have begun to walk in the path of life eternal shall continue in that path; the tongue which has sung thy praise shall never fail to sing thy truth. In the name of Jesus Christ. Amen.*

182ND DAY

NO MATTER WHAT COMES

What shall I do that I may inherit eternal life?
MARK 10:17

Read MARK 10:17-21

Be not like those who give themselves to him at one season, and withdraw from him at another. They give themselves only to be caressed; and wrest themselves back again, when they come to be crucified; or at least turn to the world for consolation. No, ye will not find consolation in aught but a free and full surrender of your will to the Divine will. Who savoureth not the cross, savoureth not the things that be of God; and a heart that savours the cross finds the bitterest things to be sweet. . . . We may be assured that there is an internal advancement, where there is an advancement in the way of [acceptance of] the cross.

PRAYER: *Into thy hands, O Lord, I commit my-self this day, and forever. Help me in all things to know thy will, and when I know it to do it gladly and perfectly, to the honor and glory of thy Name. Through Jesus Christ. Amen.*

183RD DAY

GOD'S TOUCH WITHIN US

Fear thou not; for I am with thee: be not dismayed; for I am thy God: I will strengthen thee; yea, I will help thee; yea, I will uphold thee with the right hand of my righteousness.   ISAIAH 41:10

Read ISAIAH 41:8-10

Though God gave to a man all the gifts which are possessed by all the saints, and everything that He is able to give, but withheld Himself, the gaping desire of the spirit would remain hungry and unsatisfied. The inward stirring and touching of God makes us hungry and yearning; for the Spirit of God hunts our spirit: and the more it touches it, the greater our hunger and our craving. . . . Reason can here neither give nor take away from love, for our love is touched by the Divine love. And as I understand it, here there can never more be separation from God. God's touch within us . . . and our own loving craving, these are both created and creaturely; and therefore they may grow and increase as long as we live.

PRAYER: *Infinite Father, I thank Thee for the sunshine of thy eternal remembrance and compassion. For glorious faith in the unseen God and his love, I thank Thee. Increase in me the light of the truth, I pray. And to Thee be glory. Amen.*

184TH DAY

BE HUNGRY FOR GOD

He hath filled the hungry with good things.   LUKE 1:53

Read MATTHEW 6:19-21

The rich go empty of his good things because they are filled with the food of swine. Hunger opens the storehouse of God, hunger alone. Lower things become for us evil things to choke and poison us, and to quench the longing and the taste for the food of those whose eyes, if they be lifted up, may look into the eyes of God. I have within me a deadly magic that can turn earth's beauty to a feast of rottenness wherein I lose desire for fruit of the garden of God. God is in his heaven; but He cannot force heaven into men who will not have heaven.

PRAYER: *Oh, to be made new, my God! Oh, to be changed from what I am into what I ought to be and could be! Thou who art ever making all things new, I give myself to Thee for the continual working within me of thy transforming power. Make that needed transformation to take place, Oh, my God!*

*Work within me today, so that at least some of that
transformation shall take place today. In the name
of Jesus Christ. Amen.*

A HIGHER LEVEL OF LIFE

We all, with open face beholding as in a glass the
glory of the Lord, are changed into the same image
from glory to glory.   II CORINTHIANS 3:18

Read II CORINTHIANS 3:18

There is a higher level of Christian life and
service than we are wont to recognize—a level where
self has died and disappeared and the individual
becomes God-possessed; a level where God is in
immediate control of the entire gamut of vital activities, where God is dynamically Self-expressed
through the individual. With the soul thus possessed
by divine Love there comes to the individual a
strange access of vital energy; the personality becomes dynamic; a flood of vitality seems opened that
floods the being, and lifts to a gloriously high level
of free activity every function whether of body, or
mind, or of spirit. Consciousness becomes completely
organized about the fact of God.

PRAYER: *Lift me up, O Spirit of God, to that
higher level of life in which Thou shalt be able to
express Thyself through me continually by the
words that I speak and the things that I do, and by*

all my bearing toward the people I meet. In the name of Jesus Christ. Amen.

186TH DAY

THE MAKING OF GOD IN ME

Hold that fast which thou hast, that no man take thy crown.   REVELATION 3:11

Read REVELATION 3:7-12

I am called to be the bearer of an unique incarnation, God in my own flesh. . . . The making of God in me waits only on my heart, and is the crown for me of all his miracles of love, a crown no other man may share or take away. God desires to express Himself by me as by no other man. Not I, but He living in me is the secret of love, of the love that conjoins all in one, the love that destroys self-seeking and brings forth the Self for which no life is alien. When "I" and "He" are indistinguishable for me within myself Love is incarnate in his creature, my own self; and I stand in my own place in Him bringing forth his Holy Thing that redeems.

PRAYER: *O Lord God all-glorious, who hast said that Thou wilt be unto thy people a wall of fire round about, and the glory in the midst of them, help me in all my walk day by day so to live that at least some suggestion of the fire of thy glory may go forth from me. In the name of Jesus Christ. Amen.*

THE ONE REQUIREMENT

As many as received him, to them gave he power to become the sons of God.   JOHN 1:12

Read JOHN 1:12-16

One thing is clear; God expects nothing from us save that which is in our power. He requires us to give good heed to the action of our own heart, and to his Voice speaking therein; nor is this attention hard to those who love God and wish to please Him. He requires that we should not give ourselves up to anything which is calculated to distract this attention; and so soon as we are conscious of any such distraction, He requires us to put away the cause. But do not fall into the mistake of supposing that the duties of your position, or your family, the claims of social life, or any other providential ties, need necessarily hinder this inward recollection; habit will make it part of yourself amid all outer claims.

PRAYER: *Lord, I pray Thee not for tranquillity, nor that tribulations shall cease. I ask that Thou wilt help me at all times to live in inward recollection of Thee. In the name of Jesus Christ. Amen.*

FUSION

And there appeared unto them tongues parting
asunder, like as of fire; and it sat upon each one of
them. ACTS 2:3

Read ACTS 2:1-4

How can a contact with God be in any way described? It is not seeing, but meeting and fusion
with awareness. The soul retaining her own individuality and consciousness to an intense degree,
but imbued with and fused into a life of incredible
intensity, which passes through the soul vitalities
and emotions of a life so new, so vivid, so amazing,
that she knows not whether she has been embraced
by fire, by joy, or by anguish. . . . The heat of Christ
is mixed with indescribable sweetness; giving marvellous pleasure and refreshment and happiness, and
wonderfully adapted to the delicacy of the human
creature. The heat of the Godhead is very different,
and sometimes we may even feel it to be cruel and
remorseless in its very terrible and swift intensity.
But the soul, like all great lovers, never flinches or
hangs back, but passionately lends herself.

PRAYER: *To think of Thee, the Eternal God our
Father, is to rest; to know Thee is to be possessed
of inward joy; to see Thee with the eyes of the soul
is to have the light that is at every moment needed;
to serve Thee is to have eternal life. To Thee be
glory. Amen.*

OTHER CHILDREN OF GOD

And other sheep I have, which are not of this fold: them also I must bring, and they shall hear my voice; and there shall be one fold, and one shepherd. JOHN 10:16

Read JOHN 10:14-16

In the Sufi, the Greek, the Buddhist and the Hindu, one will discover the same craving after the eternal Spirit, the same attempt to put into words that experience of Union between the soul and the Absolute. If the student has not already made this discovery two courses will be open to him when he does. He can put aside all such thought as worthless. . . . Or he can regard these thoughts which spontaneously spring up among men separated from each other by race and time, to be the normal aspiration of the human spirit towards some real object. If he chooses the second course he can gain a sympathetic understanding of the aspirations of those who in darkness, and not in vain, sought a glimmer of light.

PRAYER: *O Thou who hearest prayer, unto Thee shall all flesh come. Lead all who seek Thee anywhere, in any way, Eternal Savior, to find Thee in spirit and in truth. Amen.*

PEACE THROUGH UNION WITH GOD

He is our peace.   EPHESIANS 2:14

Read EPHESIANS 3:1-12

Feelings are very delusive. They often depend upon mere natural temperament. As men advance in the interior life, they learn to indulge less and less in self-dissection, even as regards their love of God;—they are content to give themselves up to Him in this matter as in all else—to love Him without any conscious dwelling upon their love; and this is the higher and purer form of love. It is free from all self-complacency, absorbed in God Himself. As a rule it is not well to make many conscious efforts or much self-examination with a view to increasing or preserving this love. Dwelling on the Love of God for us, a pure intention, constant self-renunciation, and faithfulness to the leadings of grace, are better means for its growth in the heart.

PRAYER: *My God! my God! Thou knowest me altogether. Thou knowest all my failures in love. But Thou knowest also that I love Thee, and that I desire to have my daily life give expression to thy nature of love. In thy service alone can I find peace. Fill me with thy love. And to Thee be glory. Amen.*

THE WAY OF INNER PEACE

My meat is to do the will of him that sent me, and
to finish his work.   JOHN 4:34

Read JOHN 4:27-34

The way of inner peace consists in conforming
ourselves in all things to the Divine Will. Those
who would have all things to succeed and come to
pass according to their own desire have not come to
know this way. This conformity is the sweet yoke
that brings us into the regions of inner peace and
serenity. Hence we may know that the rebellion of
our will is the chief cause of our disquiet; and that
because we will not submit to the sweet yoke of the
Divine Will, we suffer so many streights [*sic*] and
perturbations. O Souls! if we should submit our own
will to the Divine Will, and to all his orderings,
what tranquillity we should feel, what sweet peace,
what inward serenity, what supreme felicity and
earnest of bliss!

PRAYER: *May it please God to give me his Divine
Light, so that I might discover the Secret Paths of
this Inward Way, and the supreme Felicity of Perfect Peace. Amen.*

LET EVERYTHING REVEAL
GOD'S PRESENCE

Thou, O Lord, art our father, our redeemer; thy
name is from everlasting.   ISAIAH 63:16

Read ISAIAH 63:7-16

Let this actual thought often return, that God is
omnipresent, filling every place. Let everything you
see represent to your spirit the presence, the excel-
lency, and the power of God. In the face of the sun,
you may see God's beauty; in the fire, you may feel
his heat warming; in the water, his gentleness to
refresh you: it is the dew of heaven that makes
your field give you bread; and the breasts of God
are the bottles that minister drink to your necessities.

PRAYER: *Holy, holy, holy, Lord God Almighty,
which was, and is, and is to come: heaven and earth,
angels and men, the air and the sea, give glory and
honour and thanks to him that sitteth on the throne,
who liveth for ever and ever. Great and marvellous
are thy works, O Lord God Almighty. Thy wisdom
is infinite, thy mercies are glorious; and I am not
worthy, O Lord, to appear in thy presence, before
whom the angels hide their faces. Blessing, honour,
glory, and power be unto Him that sitteth on the
throne, and to the Lamb, for ever. Amen.*

GOD PURSUES THE SOUL

Before they call, I will answer; and while they are yet speaking, I will hear.   ISAIAH 65:24

Read ISAIAH 65:17-25

It must be known that God cometh sometimes into the soul when it hath neither called, nor prayed unto, nor summoned Him. And He doth instil into the soul a fire and a love and a sweetness not customary, wherein it doth greatly delight and rejoice; and it doth believe that this hath been wrought by God Himself there present. . . . And with that feeling whereby it is certified unto the soul that God dwelleth within it, there is given unto it a disposition so perfect that in every way do all the members of the body agree with the soul and do truly form one cause together with it; neither do they rebel against the will of the soul, but do perfectly desire those things which are of God. Thus doth the soul feel that God is mingled with it and hath made companionship with it.

PRAYER: *O Thou ever-present Creator and Savior and Friend, before it came to me to know Thee I was enfolded in thy love and life. From my earliest days Thou hast pursued me with thy Spirit. Pursue me still, O Lord, and lead me into yet deeper and more vital relations with Thee. Glory be to Thee, O Lord. Amen.*

GOD'S IMMORTAL STRENGTH

Out of weakness were made strong. HEBREWS 11:34

Read HEBREWS 11:32-40

I was suddenly called upon to pass through the valley of the shadow of death. In a moment, the dread disease of Asiatic cholera attacked me. No human aid was near at the time and it was long before a doctor could arrive. Yet Christ was intimately near me in that most desolate hour of all when I entered the dark valley, and He bade me fear no evil. For many days the awareness of any outward thing was only fitful, while I hovered between life and death. Yet the inner peace remained. A Mohammedan *khansamah*, who served me in my pain, brought very near indeed to me the love of Christ himself. For he was ever by my side comforting and supporting me. Out of that intermediate state through which I had passed for many days, I awoke at last into a new world. For when mortal weakness had reached its utmost limit, God's immortal strength had been revealed.

PRAYER: *Lord, keep me ever near to Thee; let nothing separate me from Thee; let nothing keep me back from Thee. Make me hope in Thee, trust in Thee, and love Thee everlastingly; through Jesus Christ. Amen.*

GOD LEADS TO THE LIGHT

When I fall, I shall arise.   MICAH 7:8

Read MICAH 7:7-9

Life of my life, I shall ever try to keep my body pure, knowing that thy living touch is upon all my limbs.

I shall ever try to keep all untruths out from my thoughts, knowing that Thou art that truth which has kindled the light of reason in my mind.

I shall ever try to drive all evils away from my heart and keep my love in flower, knowing that Thou hast thy seat in the inmost shrine of my heart.

And it shall be my endeavor to reveal Thee in my actions, knowing it is thy power gives me strength to act.

PRAYER: *O Thou Source of all life, who hast called thy human creatures to live as children of the resurrection, help me, thy stumbling, struggling creature, this day and every day, to lift up my thoughts and my heart to the truth and purity and love that are thy will for me. And unto Him that is able to keep me from falling, and to present me fault-less before the Presence of His glory with exceeding joy, to the only wise God our Savior, be glory and majesty, dominion and power, now and forevermore. Amen.*

NO FEAR OF DEATH

I go unto my Father.   JOHN 14:12

Read JOHN 14:1-12

As for death, it only worries carnal and worldly persons. *Perfect love casteth out fear.* It is not by believing ourselves righteous, that we cease to fear. It is simply by loving, and by yielding ourselves to the one we love without a thought of self. That is what makes death sweet and precious. When we are dead to ourselves, the death of the body is only the fulfillment of the work of grace.

PRAYER: *Almighty God, with whom do live the spirits of them that depart hence in the Lord, and with whom the souls of the faithful, after they are delivered from the burden of the flesh, are in joy and felicity: help me now, as I go from day to day, so to live that when Thou shalt call me from this life upon earth I may find perfect consummation and bliss in the eternal life that Thou hast prepared for thy people. In the name of Jesus Christ, thy Son. Amen.*

GOD'S WILL IS MY MEAT

My meat is to do the will of him that sent me, and to finish his work.   JOHN 4:34

Read JOHN 4:1-34

All men seek peace, but they seek it not where it is to be found. We fancy ourselves surrounded by a thousand urgent concerns, while there is and can be but one great interest. Where the ray of God's light shall fall upon my path, there will I walk, and, in his strength, perform, without inquietude, the work that his providence shall set before me. Peace—true peace—that which alone deserves the name—will be sought in vain by those who seek it elsewhere than in the possession of God; and that high and happy communion is to be secured and maintained only by the submission of faith, and the obedience of love. These will kindle and keep up in the heart a vestal fire of devotion to the Heavenly Father. Let us then keep untiring watch, lest we snatch at joy and grasp despair.

PRAYER: *Thou hast said it of Thyself, Lord Jesus, that, concerning thy heavenly Father, Thou didst always the things that pleased Him. Teach me, O Thou great Exemplar, to follow thy leading. With me, as it was with Thee, may it be life's great motive and object to do his will; not only in the exercises of devotion, but in all the offices of existence. Praise be to Thee, O Christ. Amen.*

THE GLORIES OF GOD

Alleluia: for the Lord God omnipotent reigneth. Let us be glad and rejoice, and give honour to him.
REVELATION 19:6, 7

Read REVELATION 19:1-10

Love is the greatest thing that God can give us: for Himself is love; and it is the greatest thing we can give to God. It is the old, and it is the new, and it is the great commandment, and it is all the commandments: for it is the fulfilling of the law. It does the work of all other graces, without any instrument but its own immediate virtue. We need no incentives to move us to the love of God; for we can not love any thing for any reason real or imaginary, but that excellence is infinitely more eminent in God. For there is in God an infinite nature, immensity or vastness without extension or limit, immutability, eternity, omnipotence, holiness, dominion, providence, bounty, mercy, justice, perfection in himself.

PRAYER: *Holy is our God; holy is the Almighty: holy is the Immortal: holy, holy, holy, Lord God of Sabaoth, heaven and earth are full of the majesty of thy glory. With these holy and blessed spirits I also, thy servant, humbly offer up my heart and voice to join in this blessed choir, and confess the glories of the Lord. To Thee be praise. Amen.*

THEE, ONLY THEE

And ye shall seek me, and find me, when ye shall search for me with all your heart.   JEREMIAH 29:13

Read JEREMIAH 29:11-13

That I want Thee, only Thee—let my heart repeat without end. All desires that distract me, day and night, are false and empty to the core.

As the night keeps hidden in its gloom the petition for light, even thus in the depth of my unconsciousness rings the cry—I want Thee, only Thee.

As the storm still seeks its end in peace when it strikes against peace with all its might, even thus my rebellion strikes against thy love and still its cry is— I want Thee, only Thee.

PRAYER: *Take me, O Lord of life, into thy keeping forever. O Thou light of lights, keep me from inward darkness. And for all the world I pray, that Thou wilt lead it out of darkness into light, till the earth shall be filled with the knowledge of the glory of the Lord, as the waters cover the sea. To Thee be praise forever. Amen.*

THE SOUL'S THIRST

O God, thou art my God; early will I seek thee: my soul thirsteth for thee, my flesh longeth for thee. PSALM 63:1

Read PSALM 63

Great art Thou, O Lord, and greatly to be praised; great is thy power, and thy wisdom infinite. And Thee would man praise; man, but a particle of thy creation; man, that bears about him his mortality, the witness of his sin, the witness that *Thou resistest the proud:* yet would man praise Thee; he, but a particle of thy creation. Thou awakest us to delight in thy praise; for Thou madest us for Thyself, and our heart is restless until it rest in Thee.

PRAYER: *Essence beyond essence, Nature increate, Framer of the world, I set Thee, Lord, before my face, and I lift up my soul unto Thee. I stretch forth my hands unto Thee, my soul is as a thirsty land towards Thee. O Lord, Thou knowest, and canst, and willest the good of my soul. Thou, O Lord, I beseech Thee, in thine unspeakable love, so order concerning me, and so dispose, as Thou knowest to be most pleasing to Thee, and most good for me. Thine is goodness, grace, love, kindness, benignity, gentleness, forbearance, longsuffering, abundant mercy, a multitude of tender mercies, a heart of compassion.*

SOURCES*

(Line 1 indicates source of meditation, followed by source of prayer)

DAY

1st W. R.
  W. R.

2nd St. Augustine, *Confessions* (*passim*)
  Lancelot Andrewes, *Preces Privatae* (adapted)

3rd Lucie Christine, *The Spiritual Journal of Lucie Christine,* ed. Rev. A. Poulain, S.J.
  W. R.

4th Auguste Sabatier
  George A. Gordon, *Revelation and the Ideal* (adapted)

5th Lucie Christine, *op. cit.* (condensed)
  Walter Rauschenbusch, *Prayers of the Social Awakening* (adapted)

6th George A. Gordon, *op. cit.*
  W. R.

7th Sadhu Sundar Singh
  Lancelot Andrewes, *op. cit.* (adapted)

8th Hallam Tennyson, *Alfred Lord Tennyson, A Memoir*
  The Golden Fountain (anonymous)

DAY

9th St. Augustine, *op. cit.*
  Lancelot Andrewes, *op. cit.*

10th Michael de Molinos, *The Spiritual Guide,* ed. Kathleen Lyttelton
  Frances Ridley Havergal

11th *Theologia Germanica,* trans. Susanna Winkworth
  W. R.

12th F. Augustine Baker, *Holy Wisdom* (condensed)
  Ibid. (condensed)

13th Lucie Christine, *op. cit.*
  Mozarabic (adapted)

14th Brother Lawrence, *The Spiritual Maxims of Brother Lawrence* (transposed)
  W. R.

15th Phillips Brooks, in A. V. G. Allen, *The Life and Letters of Phillips Brooks*
  Prayers New and Old (adapted)

16th George A. Gordon, *op. cit.* (condensed)
  Joseph Fort Newton, *Altar Stairs* (adapted)

* Every attempt has been made, on the copyright page, to acknowledge those books in copyright. If any titles have been inadvertently omitted, corrections will be made in the next edition.

17th C. F. Andrews, *Christ in the Silence*

Jeremy Taylor, *Holy Living and Dying* (in part)

18th Brother Lawrence, *op. cit.* (condensed)

Christina Rossetti (in part)

19th Frank C. Laubach, *Letters by a Modern Mystic* (condensed)

W. R.

20th Ozora S. Davis, in *Advance* (condensed)

W. R.

21st Ozora S. Davis, *loc. cit.* (condensed)

Lancelot Andrews, *op. cit.* (condensed)

22nd St. Augustine, *op. cit.*

W. R.

23rd St. Teresa of Ávila, *The Interior Castle*

Joseph Fort Newton, *Altar Stairs* (adapted)

24th Lucie Christine, *op. cit.*

Lancelot Adrewes, *op. cit.*

25th Franciscan chronicle

W. R.

26th Archbishop Fénelon, *Meditations for a Month* (condensed)

Lancelot Andrewes (altered)

27th Jane Steger, *Leaves from a Secret Journal*

W. R.

28th St. Augustine, *op. cit.*

W. R.

29th Phillips Brooks, *op. cit.*

George A. Gordon, *op. cit.* (adapted)

30th Franciscan chronicle

W. R.

31st Meister Eckhart, in *Meister Eckhart*, trans. Raymond Bernard Blakney

George A. Gordon, *op. cit.* (adapted)

32nd Meister Eckhart, *op. cit.*

W. R.

33rd Brother Lawrence, *The Practice of the Presence of God* (*passim*)

W. R.

34th Brother Lawrence, *Practice of the Presence of God*

W. E. Orchard (adapted)

35th Forbes Robinson (condensed)

W. R.

36th Meister Eckhart, *op. cit.*

Lancelot Andrewes, *op. cit.* (condensed)

37th Lucie Christine, *op. cit.*

W. R.

38th Frank C. Laubach, *op. cit.* (condensed)

Lancelot Andrewes, *op. cit.* (adapted)

39th *The Golden Fountain* (condensed)

W. R.

40th *The Golden Fountain* (condensed)

W. R.

41st Angela of Foligno, *The Book of Divine Consolation* (condensed)

W. R.

42nd Charles E. Raven, *Jesus and the Gospel of Love* (condensed)

W. H. Aitken (adapted)

43rd   Vida D. Scudder, *Saint Catherine of Siena as Seen in Her Letters* (condensed)
W. R.

44th   Sir Thomas Browne, *Religio Medici* (condensed)
Elsie Gibson (adapted)

45th   Hallam Tennyson, *op. cit.*
Henry Vaughan (adapted)

46th   Hallam Tennyson, *op. cit.* (condensed)
W. R.

47th   Evelyn Underhill
Book of Common Prayer (slightly altered)

48th   Evelyn Underhill (adapted)
W. R.

49th   *Thelogia Germanica* (condensed)
W. R.

50th   L. Adams Beck, *The Story of Oriental Philosophy* (adapted)
Toyohiko Kagawa (adapted)

51st   Thomas R. Kelly, *A Testament of Devotion*
George A. Gordon, *op. cit.* (adapted)

52nd   Forbes Robinson (in a letter)
Adapted from a common prayer

53rd   Forbes Robinson (in a letter)
W. R.

54th   St. Teresa of Ávila, *op. cit.* (transposed)
W. R.

55th   Thomas R. Kelly, *op. cit.* (condensed)
W. R.

56th   Thomas R. Kelly, *op. cit.*
W. R.

57th   Hallam Tennyson, *op. cit.*
W. R.

58th   Thomas R. Kelly, *op. cit.*
W. R.

59th   St. Teresa of Ávila, *op. cit.*
Adapted

60th   Rufus M. Jones, *The Trail of Life in College*
George A. Gordon, *op. cit.* (adapted)

61st   Franklyn Cole Sherman, *Religion Applied to Life*
W. R.

62nd   Phillips Brooks, *op. cit.*
W. R.

63rd   Rufus M. Jones, *op. cit.*
W. R.

64th   Hallam Tennyson, *op. cit.*
W. R.

65th   Forbes Robinson (condensed)
W. R.

66th   Frank C. Laubach, *op. cit.* (condensed)
W. R.

67th   St. Augustine, *op. cit.*
George A. Gordon, *op. cit.* (adapted)

68th   In Piero Misciattelli, *The Mystics of Siena*
Thomas à Kempis

69th   Paul Dubois, *The Psychic Treatment of Nervous Disorders*
Adapted

70th   Epictetus
        George A. Gordon, *op.
        cit.* (adapted)
71st   Zephine Humphrey, *The
        Beloved Community*
        W. R.
72nd   Jane Steger, *op. cit.*
        (condensed)
        W. R.
73rd   Thomas R. Kelly, *op.
        cit.*
        Gelasian Sacramentary
        (altered)
74th   *The Golden Fountain*
        (condensed)
        *Prayers for Private De-
        votions* (adapted)
75th   F. W. Robertson, *Ser-
        mons*
        W. R.
76th   St. Augustine, *op. cit.*
        W. R.
77th   Brother Lawrence, *Prac-
        tice of the Presence of
        God* (*passim*)
        W. R.
78th   Brother Lawrence, *Prac-
        tice of the Presence of
        God* (condensed)
        Adapted
79th   *The Golden Fountain*
        (condensed)
        W. R.
80th   Lucie Christine, *op. cit.*
        W. R.
81st   Julian of Norwich, *Reve-
        lations of Divine Love*,
        ed. Dom Roger Hud-
        leston
        St. Francis of Assisi
82nd   Vida D. Scudder, *op.
        cit.*
        W. R.
83th   Julian of Norwich, *op.
        cit.* (condensed)
        W. R.

84th   Jane Steger, *op. cit.*
        E. B. Pusey (adapted)
85th   Brother Lawrence, *Prac-
        tice of the Presence of
        God* (*passim*)
        Adapted
86th   Brother Lawrence, *Prac-
        tice of the Presence of
        God* (condensed)
        Adapted
87th   Thomas R. Kelly, *op.
        cit.*
        Liturgy of St. James
        (adapted)
88th   *Theologia Germanica*
        W. R.
89th   Zephine Humphrey, *op.
        cit.* (condensed)
        George Dawson (con-
        densed)
90th   Charles E. Raven, *A
        Wanderer's Way* (con-
        densed)
        W. R.
91st   Jane Steger, *op. cit.*
        (condensed)
        W. R.
92nd   Lucie Christine, *op. cit.*
        (transposed)
        W. R.
93rd   *The Golden Fountain*
        (condensed)
        Lucie Christine, *op. cit.*
        (altered)
94th   Lucie Christine, *op. cit.*
        (condensed)
        W. R.
95th   W. R.
        W. R.
96th   *Theologia Germanica*
        (condensed)
        W. R.
97th   Brother Lawrence, *Prac-
        tice of the Presence of
        God* (condensed)
        W. R.

98th Michael de Molinos, *op. cit.* (slightly altered) Adapted

99th Albert Schweitzer, *Out of My Life and Thought* (condensed) W. R.

100th *Theologia Germanica* W. R.

101st Charles E. Raven, *A Wanderer's Way* (condensed) W. R.

102nd Jane Steger, *op. cit.* (condensed) W. R.

103rd W. Scott Palmer, *A Modern Mystic's Way* (condensed) W. R.

104th Marjorie Sykes, *Rabindranath Tagore* W. R.

105th Baron Friedrich von Hügel W. R.

106th Meister Eckhart, *op. cit.* (*passim*) Lancelot Andrewes, *op. cit.* (condensed and changed to first person)

107th Lucie Christine, *op. cit.* (condensed) W. R.

108th Forbes Robinson W. R.

109th Meister Eckhart, *op. cit.* George A. Gordon, *op. cit.*

110th Epictetus George A. Gordon, *op. cit.* (adapted)

111th F. W. Robertson, *op. cit.* Lancelot Andrewes, *op. cit.*

112th Cotton Mather (in his diary, 1711, after thirty years in the ministry) George A. Gordon, *op. cit.* (altered)

113th Jane Steger, *op. cit.* St. Benedict

114th Julian of Norwich, *op. cit.* (condensed) Adapted

115th Count Leo Tolstoy Henry Ward Beecher (modified)

116th W. R. (retold) W. R.

117th William James, in *The Letters of William James,* ed. Henry James W. R.

118th *The Cloud of Unknowing* (par. 1) ; St. Teresa of Ávila, *op. cit.* (par. 2) ; Johann Kepler (par. 3) W. R.

119th W. R. W. R.

120th Thomas R. Kelly, *op. cit.* (condensed) W. R.

121st Frank C. Laubach, *op. cit.* (condensed) W. R.

122nd Sir Thomas Browne, *op. cit.* Lancelot Andrewes, *op. cit.* (condensed)

123rd Meister Eckhart, *op. cit.* Altered

124th Sir Thomas Browne, *op. cit.* (*passim*) Adapted

125th Julian of Norwich, *op. cit.*

Prayers for Students (adapted)

126th *Theologia Germanica* (condensed)

Lucie Christine, *op. cit.*

127th Jane Steger, *op. cit.* (condensed)
W. R.

128th Brother Lawrence, *Spiritual Maxims*
W. R.

129th W. R.
W. R.

130th Archbishop Fénelon, *op. cit.* (condensed)
W. R.

131st Brother Lawrence, *Spiritual Maxims* (condensed)
Ibid. (condensed)

132nd *Ibid.* (condensed)
W. R.

133rd Abraham Joshua Heschel, *Man Is Not Alone*
W. R.

134th Julian of Norwich, *op. cit.*
W. R.

135th *The Cloud of Unknowing* (*passim*)
W. R.

136th Meister Eckhart, *op. cit.* (*passim*)
W. R.

137th *Theologia Germanica* (condensed)
St. Augustine, *op. cit.* (altered)

138th Meister Eckhart, *op. cit.*
Lancelot Andrewes, *op. cit.* (in part)

139th Rufus M. Jones, *The Trail of Life in the Middle Years* (*passim*)

Altered from a common prayer

140th Abraham Joshua Heschel, *op. cit.*

Lancelot Andrewes, *op. cit.* (adapted)

141st *Theologia Germanica*
Slightly altered from a common prayer

142nd Thomas R. Kelly, *op. cit.* (condensed)

Lancelot Andrewes, *op. cit.* (condensed)

143rd *The Cloud of Unknowing* (condensed)
W. R.

144th Meister Eckhart, *op. cit.*
W. R.

145th Richard Rolle, *The Fire of Love* (condensed)
Ibid.

146th *Ibid.* (condensed)
W. R.

147th H. L. Sidney Lear, *The Hidden Life of the Soul* (based on Jean Nicolas Grou (condensed)

Julia Lee Rubel (adapted)

148th John of Ruysbroeck, *The Adornment of the Spiritual Marriage*

Lancelot Andrewes, *op. cit.*

149th William Law, *Selected Spiritual Writings,* ed. Stephen Hobhouse
Adapted

150th *The Cloud of Unknowing* (condensed)

Lancelot Andrewes, *op. cit.* (adapted)

151st Julian of Norwich, *op. cit.*
Adapted

152nd John of Ruysbroeck, *op. cit.* (condensed)
W. R.

153rd Sadhu Sundar Singh (condensed)
Coptic Liturgy of St. Basil (adapted)

154th W. Scott Palmer, *op. cit.* (condensed)
W. R.

155th H. L. Sidney Lear, *op. cit.* (condensed)
W. R.

156th Meister Eckhart, *op. cit.*
W. R.

157th *A Guide to True Peace* (condensed)
W. R.

158th F. Augustine Baker, *op. cit.*
Ibid.

159th *Ibid.* (condensed)
Ibid. (adapted)

160th William Law, *op. cit.* (condensed)
W. R.

161st *The Cloud of Unknowing* (*passim*)
W. R.

162nd *The Mirror of Simple Souls*, ed. Clare Kirchberger
Bishop Charles Henry Brent

163rd William Law, *op. cit.* (condensed)
W. R.

164th *A Guide to True Peace* Adapted

165th F. Augustine Baker, *op. cit.* (condensed)
Ibid. (selected)

166th Julian of Norwich, *op. cit.*
W. R.

167th H. L. Sidney Lear, *op. cit.* (condensed)
W. R.

168th Sadhu Sundar Singh (condensed)
W. R.

169th George A. Gordon, *op. cit.*
W. R.

170th William Law, *op. cit.* Adapted

171st Chuang Tsu (par. 1); Richard of St. Victor (par. 2); Meister Eckhart, *op. cit.* (par. 3)
W. R.

172nd Frank C. Laubach, *op. cit.*
W. R.

173rd F. Augustine Baker, *op. cit.* (arranged)
Joseph Fort Newton, *Altar Stairs* (slightly altered)

174th William Law, *op. cit.* (condensed)
W. R.

175th *A Guide to True Peace* (condensed)
W. R.

176th William Law, *op. cit.* (condensed)
Lancelot Andrewes, *op. cit.* (condensed)

177th Kathleen Lyttelton
W. R.

178th W. Scott Palmer, *op. cit.* Adapted

179th William Law, *op. cit.* Adapted

180th W. Scott Palmer, *op. cit.* (condensed)
Phillips Brooks, *op. cit.* (changed to first person)

181st John of Ruysbroeck, *op. cit.*
W. R.

182nd *A Guide to True Peace*
Adapted

183rd John of Ruysbroeck, *op. cit.*
George A. Gordon, *op. cit.* (altered)

184th W. Scott Palmer, *op. cit.* (condensed)
W. R.

185th Laird Wingate Snell (condensed)
W. R.

186th W. Scott Palmer, *op. cit.* (condensed)
W. R.

187th H. L. Sidney Lear, *op. cit.* (condensed)
Based on Savonarola

188th *The Golden Fountain* (condensed)
W. R.

189th C. F. Kelley, in his Introduction to *The Book of the Poor in Spirit* (anonymous)
W. R.

190th H. L. Sidney Lear, *op. cit.* (condensed)
W. R.

191st Michael de Molinos, *op. cit.* (condensed)
Ibid.

192nd Jeremy Taylor, *op. cit.* (condensed)
Ibid. (condensed)

193rd Angela of Foligno, *op. cit.* (condensed)
W. R.

194th C. F. Andrews, *op. cit.* (condensed)
E. B. Pusey (condensed and changed to first person)

195th Rabindranath Tagore, *Gitanjali*
W. R.

196th Archbishop Fénelon, *op. cit.*
Altered

197th Archbishop Fénelon, *op. cit.* (*passim*)
Adapted

198th Jeremy Taylor, *op. cit.* (condensed)
Ibid. (abbreviated)

199th Rabindranath Tagore, *op. cit.*
Adapted

200th St. Augustine, *op. cit.*
Lancelot Andrewes, *op. cit.* (condensed)

Set in Fairfield
Format by Terry Pace
Manufactured by The Haddon Craftsmen, Inc.
Published by HARPER & BROTHERS, *New York*